LEAN CUISINE

LEAN CUISINE

ANNE AGER

OCTOPUS BOOKS

ACKNOWLEDGMENTS

photography:
Graham Kirk
photographic styling:
Antonia Gaunt
food prepared for photography:
Anne Ager
illustrations:
Alison Wisenfeld
editors:
Piers Murray Hill
Moyra Fraser
art director:
Jane Willis
designer:
Michelle Stamp
front cover:
Scallopines of Salmon with
Raspberry Vinegar

NOTES

Standard spoon measurements are used in all the recipes.
1 tablespoon = one 15 ml spoon
1 teaspoon   = one 5 ml spoon
All spoon measures are level unless otherwise stated.

For all recipes, quantities are given in metric and imperial. Follow one set of measures only as they are not interchangeable.

Fresh herbs are used unless otherwise stated.
If unobtainable substitute dried herbs but halve the quantities stated.

First published 1986
by Octopus Books Limited
59 Grosvenor Street, London W1

© 1986 Octopus Books Limited

ISBN 0 7064 2658 4

Printed in Hong Kong

Contents

*L*ean Cuisine is a book about good food with style — not food that is just visually appealing, but food that is also good for you. It is the gourmet approach to everyday healthy eating. The dishes have all the virtues of beautiful classic cooking, and yet are healthier for you.

Our taste in food and our attitudes towards eating have changed quite dramatically: we now prefer lighter textures and fresher flavours, and we recognize the need to improve our diets by eating less fat, sugar and salt, and more dietary fibre. In addition, it has now become popular to regard food as an 'edible art form'. All the recipes I have created especially for *Lean Cuisine* reflect these trends.

Lean Cuisine shows just how easy it is to prepare food, both for family meals and for entertaining, that is satisfying both to the eye and the palate. The recipes have been written in such a way that the preparation, cooking and final serving are made as effortless as possible.

Meticulous planning is one of the secrets of any successful and memorable meal. Great care should be taken to arrange a well-balanced menu. You should try to avoid duplicating flavours, colours and textures in the different dishes; the components of the meal should complement each other perfectly.

If the main dish is rather substantial, choose something really light as a starter; equally, a small salad offered after such a dish helps to refresh the palate.

The criterion of healthy eating has been rigorously applied to all the recipes, but *Lean Cuisine* is not a punishment cookbook! Your family and friends will really enjoy the food: soups thickened naturally by vegetables; sauces based on fromage blanc or yogurt rather than cream; unusual salads with equally interesting dressings; fish cooked with little or no fat and a variety of fresh herbs; chicken, veal and rabbit dishes with some very original sauces; wholemeal pasta and brown rice dishes, fragrant with herbs and spices; and even delectable desserts, comparatively low in calories. Throughout I have used low-fat cooking techniques, such as poaching, steaming or baking in foil parcels.

The stunning photographs emphasize the importance of presenting food attractively. The ideas for garnishing and decorating are quick and simple, and I know that you can achieve the same effects as I have. The Cook's Tips will encourage the less experienced of you to be more adventurous, and you will see from the variations suggested in each recipe how easy it is to expand your repertoire.

Lean Cuisine is very practical and I can guarantee that all the recipes are easy to make. Many of the dishes are of course suitable for serving at dinner parties, but this is essentially a book for everyday use and enjoyment.

Starters

A starter is the scene-setter of a meal and, for this reason alone, should reflect the style and standard of what is to follow. Any first course should be a light introduction to the following courses, titillating the appetite rather than satisfying it. You will see that the appetizer portions in this chapter are fairly small.

When choosing a starter, always bear in mind the flavour, colour and texture of the others courses so that you can avoid repetition. It is better to choose dishes which do not have very predominant flavours; avoid, for example, strong spices such as chilli, cumin and turmeric.

The beginning of any meal is the busiest time for the cook or hostess. Not only is there the starter to serve, but a final check has to be made that everything for the main course can look after itself in the kitchen, while you sit down at the table. This is a very good reason for choosing a starter that can be prepared in advance and placed on the table before you gather your guests to the dining room. If you are really determined to serve a hot, 'last minute' starter, then you should plan a relatively effortless main course.

You will find a variety of ideas here, all of which are a welcome break away from the all-too-popular prawn cocktail or minestrone soup. Most of them are very light, ranging from chilled soups to little warm Tarts of Parma Ham and Mustard. Tomato and Basil Sorbet is refreshing on a hot summer's day, while Cheese and Herb Roulade is more appropriate when there is a distinct nip in the air.

You can really go to town with the garnish for starters. Many of them are served on fish plates (about 20 cm/8 inch in diameter) which allows plenty of space for julienne strips of vegetables, fresh herbs or decoratively cut slices of citrus fruit.

TOMATO AND COURGETTE SOUP

preparation: 25 minutes, plus chilling

cooking: 15 minutes

serves 4

•

900 g/2 lb tomatoes, skinned,
seeded and chopped

3 tablespoons olive oil

1 garlic clove, peeled and crushed

1 tablespoon chopped basil

600 ml/1 pint chicken stock (page 137)

salt and freshly ground black pepper

4 medium courgettes, topped, tailed and
coarsely shredded

4 ice cubes

to garnish (optional):

3 tablespoons homemade yogurt (page 139)

small sprigs of fresh basil

1 Cook the tomatoes gently in the olive oil with the garlic for 10 minutes.
2 Add the basil, stock, and salt and pepper to taste; simmer for 5 minutes.
3 Blend the soup in a liquidizer or food processor until fairly smooth. Cool.
4 Stir the courgettes into the soup; cover and chill for 4 hours.
5 Ladle into shallow soup bowls and add an ice cube to each one.
6 Swirl a little yogurt onto each portion and garnish with a sprig of basil, if liked.

Cook's Tip If the courgettes are prepared with the shredder blade of a food processor, the soup will have a better texture; alternatively, use the coarse side of a grater. The longer the soup is chilled, the better the flavour; if you have the time, make it the night before.

Variation If you have a little leftover white wine, substitute it for some of the stock. This soup can also be served hot with Dry-bake Herb Croûtons (page 140).

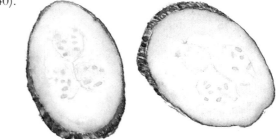

CHILLED CONSOMME JULIENNE

preparation: 15 minutes, plus chilling

cooking: 2 minutes

serves 4

•

1 medium carrot, peeled and cut into
matchstick strips

1 red pepper, cored, seeded and cut into
matchstick strips

2 spring onions, topped, tailed, and cut
into matchstick strips

600 ml/1 pint chicken stock (page 137)

3 tablespoons dry sherry

2 teaspoons powdered gelatine

2 tablespoons water

2 tablespoons crème fraîche

1 tablespoon chopped chives

paprika

1 Blanch the strips of vegetable in boiling water for 1−2 minutes; drain and refresh immediately in very cold water.
2 Mix the stock with the sherry.
3 Mix the gelatine with the water in a small bowl and set aside for 1 minute. Stand in a pan of hot water and leave until the gelatine has dissolved, about 2 minutes.
4 Add the dissolved gelatine to the stock and chill until syrupy.
5 Add the cooked strips of vegetable to the syrupy stock and pour into four soup bowls. Chill until just set.
6 Spoon a little crème fraîche on top of each portion and sprinkle with chives and paprika. Serve immediately with small triangles of lightly buttered wholemeal bread.

Cook's Tip You can, if necessary, use 600 ml/1 pint of a good canned consommé in place of the homemade chicken stock set with gelatine; and still add the sherry.

Variation Top each portion with homemade yogurt (page 139) and black lumpfish roe instead of crème fraîche and chives.

Tomato and Courgette Soup: *A fresh-tasting tomato soup delicately flavoured with basil and finished with colourful shreds of courgette.*

AVOCADO AND MINT SOUP

preparation: 10 minutes, plus chilling
serves 4

2 ripe avocados, halved, stoned and peeled

grated rind and juice of ½ lemon

3 spring onions, topped, tailed
and chopped

1 garlic clove, peeled and chopped

400 ml/14 fl oz chicken stock (page 137)

150 ml/¼ pint homemade yogurt (page 139)

salt and freshly ground black pepper

1 tablespoon chopped mint

to garnish:

sprigs of fresh mint

1 Chop the avocado flesh into a liquidizer or food processor.
2 Add the lemon rind and juice, spring onions, garlic, stock, yogurt, salt and pepper to taste and the mint; blend until smooth.
3 Cover the soup and chill for 4 hours, or overnight.
4 Spoon into small glass bowls and garnish each portion with a sprig of fresh mint.

Cook's Tip If you are chilling the soup overnight, put the avocado stones in the soup and cover it with cling film – this will help to prevent the soup from losing its fresh green colour.
Variation This soup is delicious if it is lightly spiced – add about ½ teaspoon curry powder (page 141).

CHILLED SPANISH VEGETABLE SOUP

preparation: 15 minutes, plus chilling
serves 4

450 g/1 lb tomatoes, skinned

300 ml/½ pint chicken stock (page 137)

2 garlic cloves, peeled

3 tablespoons olive oil

1 medium onion, peeled and thinly sliced

½ cucumber, halved, seeded and very
finely chopped

1 medium red pepper, cored, seeded and
very finely chopped

salt and freshly ground black pepper

3 tablespoons chopped parsley

coarsely crushed ice

1 Put the tomatoes, chicken stock, garlic and olive oil into a liquidizer or food processor; blend until smooth.
2 Pour the tomato mixture into a bowl and stir in the onion, cucumber and red pepper, salt and pepper to taste, and 2 tablespoons of the parsley.
3 Cover the soup and chill very thoroughly for 3–4 hours.
4 Serve in small glass bowls, adding a good tablespoon of ice to each one and sprinkle with the remaining parsley.
5 Serve immediately, either with pieces of wholemeal bread, or with Dry-bake Herb Croûtons (page 140).

Cook's Tip Use the large Continental tomatoes if you can obtain them; they give the soup a much better flavour.
Variation Sprinkle 2 finely chopped, hard-boiled eggs over the soup just before serving, if you want to make it a little more substantial.

SPICED APRICOT SOUP WITH TOASTED ALMONDS

preparation: 20 minutes, plus chilling

serves 4

●

450 g/1 lb fresh ripe apricots

400 ml/14 fl oz dry white wine

grated rind and juice of ½ orange

200 ml/⅓ pint homemade yogurt (page 139)

3 tablespoons flaked almonds, toasted

ground mixed spice or nutmeg

1 Make a nick in the stalk end of each apricot; put the fruit into a bowl and cover with boiling water for 1 minute. Drain the apricots and remove the skins.
2 Halve and stone the apricots and put them into a liquidizer or food processor.
3 Add half the white wine and blend to a purée. Gradually blend in the remaining white wine, the orange rind and juice, the yogurt and 2 tablespoons of the almonds. Blend until smooth.
4 Cover the soup and chill for 4 hours, or overnight.
5 Serve in small soup bowls, sprinkled with the remaining almonds and a little mixed spice or nutmeg.

Cook's Tip If fresh apricots are out of season, you can use canned ones, provided they are preserved in natural juice or apple juice, and not in syrup. Do not waste the juice; drink it chilled for breakfast.
Variation Other summer fruits like peaches, strawberries and cherries also make delicious fruit soups.

CURRIED SALMON BISQUE

preparation: 30 minutes

cooking: 50 minutes

serves 4

●

1 small tail end of salmon (about 450 g/1 lb)

few sprigs of fennel

1 small onion, peeled and thinly sliced

2 strips lemon peel

600 ml/1 pint water

300 ml/½ pint dry white wine

1 bay leaf

15 g/½ oz butter

1½ tablespoons wholemeal flour

salt and freshly ground black pepper

2 teaspoons curry powder (page 141)

2 teaspoons orange lumpfish roe

3 tablespoons crème fraîche

3 tablespoons dry vermouth

1 Put the salmon into a pan with the fennel, onion, lemon peel, water, white wine and bay leaf; cover and simmer gently for 10 minutes until the salmon is just tender.
2 Lift out the piece of salmon carefully; ease off the skin and then remove all the flesh in neat flakes.
3 Return the salmon skin and the bones to the pan and continue simmering gently for a further 30 minutes. Strain the salmon stock.
4 Melt the butter in a pan; add the flour and cook for 1 minute. Gradually stir in the salmon stock and bring to the boil, stirring.
5 Add salt and pepper to taste and the curry powder, and simmer for 5 minutes.
6 Stir in the flaked salmon, lumpfish roe, crème fraîche and vermouth, and heat through gently.
7 Serve piping hot.

Cook's Tip When making the stock, it is worth cooking a larger piece of salmon than the quantity given, as you will then have some cooked salmon to use for another dish.
Variation A more economical fish bisque can be made using monkfish; add some other fish bones when making the stock to give extra flavour.

ARTICHOKE AND CHICKEN LIVER SOUP

preparation: 15 minutes

cooking: 30 minutes

serves 4

1 small onion, peeled and finely chopped

1 tablespoon olive oil

1 garlic clove, peeled and crushed

100 g/4 oz chicken livers, chopped

2 × 400 g/14 oz cans artichoke hearts

chicken stock (page 137)

150 ml/¼ pint dry white wine

salt and freshly ground black pepper

3 tablespoons crème fraîche

1 tablespoon chopped parsley

1 Fry the onion gently in the oil for 3 minutes; add the garlic and chopped chicken livers and fry gently for a further 3 minutes.

2 Drain off the liquid from the artichoke hearts; make up to 600 ml/1 pint with chicken stock.

3 Add the artichoke liquid and stock mixture to the fried onion and chicken livers, together with all but two of the artichoke hearts, the white wine, and salt and pepper to taste. Bring to the boil and simmer for 20 minutes.

4 Blend the soup in a liquidizer or food processor until smooth; blend in the crème fraîche.

5 Chop the remaining artichoke hearts.

6 Transfer the soup to a clean saucepan; add the parsley and artichoke hearts and heat through.

7 Serve with Dry-bake Herb Croûtons (page 140).

Cook's Tip It is very easy to adjust the consistency of this soup to taste. For a thicker soup, reduce the quantity of stock and artichoke liquid; there will still be sufficient to serve four, as a thicker soup is more satisfying.

Variation Chicken livers give the soup quite a pronounced flavour; for a milder taste use chopped, boned and skinned chicken instead.

PARMA HAM AND MUSTARD TARTS

preparation: 20 minutes

cooking: 25 minutes

oven temperature: 190°C, 375°F, Gas Mark 5

serves 6

350 g/12 oz prepared weight Lean Pastry (page 140)

beaten egg

filling:

100 g/4 oz lean Parma ham, chopped

175 g/6 oz fromage blanc (page 140)

1 teaspoon French mustard

3 eggs

salt and freshly ground black pepper

4 tablespoons dry vermouth

2 teaspoons pesto sauce

to garnish:

sprigs of fresh basil

1 Roll out the pastry quite thinly and use to line six individual loose-bottomed tartlet tins, about 9 cm/3½ inch in diameter. Press up the pastry edges well.

2 Glaze the pastry edges with beaten egg; line each pastry case with a circle of foil or greaseproof paper and fill with a few baking beans.

3 Bake the pastry cases blind in the preheated oven for 10 minutes.

4 Meanwhile prepare the filling: mix the Parma ham with the fromage blanc and the mustard; beat in the eggs, salt and pepper to taste, vermouth and pesto sauce.

5 Remove the beans and paper from each pastry case and spoon in some of the prepared filling, dividing it evenly between the pastry cases.

6 Return to the oven for a further 15 minutes until the pastry is golden and the filling just set.

7 Garnish with sprigs of basil and serve warm with a small bowl of Mustard Fruit Pickle (page 141), if liked.

Cook's Tip Lean Pastry is a little more difficult to handle than ordinary shortcrust pastry; chill the pastry well before using and keep it as cool as possible while rolling it out.

Variation Spinach and curd cheese make a delicious savoury filling, seasoned well, and bound with a little beaten egg; alternatively, try flaked cooked fish with peeled prawns, eggs, quark and a little grated Parmesan cheese.

Parma Ham and Mustard Tarts: *Small crisp cases of lean pastry*
contain a delicious warm filling of Parma Ham, fromage blanc and mustard.

HOT CRAB AND AVOCADO SOUFFLES

preparation: 20 minutes

cooking: 25 minutes

oven temperature: 190°C, 375°F, Gas Mark 5

serves 4

15 g/½ oz butter

1 tablespoon wholemeal flour

150 ml/¼ pint skimmed milk

salt and freshly ground black pepper

½ teaspoon finely grated lemon rind

3 eggs, separated

175 g/6 oz white crabmeat, fresh or frozen

1 avocado (just ripe), halved, stoned, peeled and chopped

1 Grease four individual soufflé dishes, about 9 cm/3½ inch in diameter.
2 Melt the butter and stir in the flour; cook for 30 seconds. Gradually add the skimmed milk and bring to the boil, stirring, until the sauce has thickened.
3 Add salt and pepper to taste and the lemon rind, and beat in the egg yolks.
4 Whisk the egg whites until stiff but not dry. Mix the crabmeat into the sauce mixture and then lightly fold in the avocado and the egg whites.
5 Divide the mixture between the prepared soufflé dishes. Bake in the preheated oven for 25 minutes or until well risen and golden.
6 Serve immediately.

Cook's Tip It is important to make sure that the avocado is still slightly firm, otherwise it will become mushy when cooked.
Variation Canned salmon or tuna fish (well drained) can be used in place of the crabmeat.

EGG SCRAMBLE WITH SMOKED FISH

preparation: 10 minutes

cooking: 3−4 minutes

serves 4

4 eggs

salt and freshly ground black pepper

2 tablespoons homemade yogurt (page 139)

1 tablespoon chopped chives

225 g/8 oz thinly sliced smoked halibut or smoked salmon

25 g/1 oz butter

4 teaspoons black lumpfish roe

1 Beat the eggs with salt and pepper to taste, the yogurt and chopped chives.
2 Arrange the smoked fish on four individual plates, leaving a small space in the centre of each one.
3 Heat the butter gently in a pan until melted; add the beaten egg mixture and cook over a low heat until the egg forms soft creamy flakes.
4 Spoon into the centre of each plate of smoked fish and top with a little black lumpfish roe.
5 Serve immediately before the lumpfish roe has a chance to discolour the scrambled egg.

Cook's Tip Scrambled egg has a particularly good consistency if it is cooked in the top of a double saucepan; alternatively, use a saucepan which has a heavy base, so that the egg does not cook too quickly.
Variation Smoked haddock, which has been poached and flaked, can be served hot in the same way.

TUNA AND TWO BEAN SALAD

preparation: 20 minutes
serves 4

●

1 × 425 g/15 oz can red kidney beans

1 × 425 g/15 oz can cannellini beans

1 small onion, peeled and thinly sliced

1 small red or yellow pepper, cored, seeded
and cut into matchstick strips

3 tablespoons olive oil

1 tablespoon lemon juice

1 tablespoon tarragon vinegar

salt and freshly ground black pepper

2 garlic cloves, peeled and crushed

1 × 200 g/7 oz can tuna fish in brine,
drained and coarsely flaked

leaves of radicchio

1 Rinse both varieties of canned beans and drain thoroughly – this gets rid of the excess starch.
2 Mix the drained beans in a bowl with the onion and matchstick strips of pepper.
3 Mix the oil, lemon juice, vinegar, salt and pepper to taste, and the garlic together for the dressing.
4 Stir the dressing into the beans, adding the flaked tuna; do not overmix at this stage.
5 Serve in small bowls, lined with radicchio leaves.

Cook's Tip Use dried beans when you have the time, but remember that all dried beans require pre-soaking and must be boiled for the first 10 minutes of cooking time.
Variation Small squares of lean Parma ham make a delicious addition to this salad, in place of the flaked tuna.

A MIXED SMOKED PLATTER

preparation: 15 minutes
serves 4

●

2 small smoked mackerel fillets

1 piece smoked cod's roe (about 175 g/6 oz)

100 g/4 oz smoked salmon, thinly sliced

finely shredded lettuce or chicory

3 tablespoons homemade yogurt (page 139)

1 tablespoon freshly grated horseradish

salt and freshly ground black pepper
(optional)

to garnish:

thin wedges of lemon

feathery sprigs of dill or fennel

1 Remove the smoked mackerel flesh from the skin in fairly thick flakes. Cut the smoked cod's roe into thin slices, retaining the skin.
2 Arrange the smoked mackerel, smoked cod's roe and smoked salmon on beds of lettuce or chicory on four individual plates.
3 Mix the yogurt with the horseradish (adding salt and pepper to taste, if you feel it is necessary), and spoon a little into the centre of each arrangement of fish.
4 Garnish with wedges of lemon and sprigs of dill or fennel and serve with small triangles of lightly buttered wholemeal bread.

Cook's Tip If you want to keep the cost of this starter down, use smoked salmon offcuts which are much cheaper than the sliced variety.
Variation Look out for smoked halibut; it is now available from several fishmongers and is a delicious alternative to smoked salmon. If you can get hold of samphire (an edible seaweed), it makes a very pretty garnish and is extremely good to eat.

SPINACH AND FISH TERRINE

preparation: 35 minutes, plus chilling

cooking: 6 minutes

serves 4

8–10 well-shaped young spinach leaves

4 small single fillets of sole, skinned

1 tablespoon chopped parsley

finely grated rind of ½ lemon

salt and freshly ground black pepper

200 ml/⅓ pint dry white wine

1 × 200 g/7 oz can tuna fish in brine, drained

100 g/4 oz well-drained, cooked spinach

150 ml/¼ pint homemade yogurt (page 139)

100 g/4 oz cooked, peeled prawns

3 teaspoons powdered gelatine

3 tablespoons dry vermouth

to garnish:

thin wedges of lemon, or

feathery sprigs of fennel

1 Grease and line a 450 g/1 lb loaf tin or terrine with non-stick silicone or greased greaseproof paper.
2 Remove any tough stalk from each spinach leaf; blanch in boiling water for about 30 seconds and then immediately refresh in cold water. Drain thoroughly and spread out flat.
3 Line the prepared loaf tin or terrine with some of the spinach leaves; reserve two for covering the top of the mixture.
4 Spread out the fillets of sole, skin-side uppermost; sprinkle with parsley, lemon rind, and salt and pepper to taste. Roll up neatly like Swiss rolls and secure each one with a wooden cocktail stick.
5 Place the rolled fillets in a small shallow pan; add the wine and salt and pepper to taste, and poach, covered, for 5 minutes.
6 Remove the cooked fillets and reserve the cooking liquid.
7 Put the tuna fish, blanched spinach, yogurt, half the peeled prawns and the fish cooking liquid into a liquidizer or food processor; blend until smooth and add salt and pepper to taste.
8 Put the gelatine and vermouth into a small bowl and set aside for 1 minute. Stand in a pan of hot water and leave until the gelatine has dissolved, about 2 minutes. Stir into the tuna and spinach mixture, together with the remaining prawns.
9 Spread half the tuna and spinach mixture into the prepared loaf tin or terrine; lay the cooked sole fillets on the mixture and cover with the remaining tuna and spinach mixture.
10 Cover and chill for 3–4 hours. Unmould carefully.
11 Cut into fairly thin slices; arrange two slices on each plate and trickle over a little Herb and Lemon Sauce (page 138). Garnish with the lemon wedges or fennel sprigs.

Cook's Tip Line the two long sides and the base of the terrine with a strip of non-stick silicone or greased greaseproof paper, so that it overlaps the edges of the tin. The paper can then be used to unmould the terrine easily.
Variation Canned salmon can be used in place of canned tuna, and crème fraîche can be used instead of yogurt to give a slightly richer flavour.

SMOKED COD'S ROE MOUSSE

preparation: 15 minutes, plus chilling

serves 4

175 g/6 oz smoked cod's roe, skinned

75 g/3 oz curd cheese

finely grated rind of ½ lemon

salt and freshly ground black pepper

2 tablespoons olive oil

2 hard-boiled eggs

1 tablespoon coarsely chopped parsley

to garnish:

coarsely chopped parsley

1 Put the cod's roe into a liquidizer or food processor with the curd cheese, lemon rind, salt and pepper to taste and the olive oil; blend until smooth.
2 Separate the yolks from the whites of the hard-boiled eggs; add the yolks to the cod's roe mixture and blend until smooth.
3 Chop the egg whites finely; stir into the cod's roe mixture, together with the parsley. Cover and chill for 1–2 hours.
4 Serve on small plates in neat scoops, sprinkled with parsley and accompanied by fingers of warm wholemeal toast.

Cook's Tip This mousse is very rich, and this recipe makes a relatively small amount; the quantity of cod's roe and curd cheese can be increased slightly.
Variation Other smoked fish such as mackerel or trout can be used in place of the cod's roe.

Spinach and Fish Terrine: *Rolled fillets of sole nestle inside a prawn and tuna mousse; all enclosed in fresh spinach leaves.*

PRAWN AND LETTUCE MOUSSE

preparation: 20 minutes, plus chilling

serves 4

175 g/6 oz cooked, peeled prawns

150 ml/¼ pint fish stock (page 137)

150 ml/¼ pint homemade yogurt (page 139)

2 teaspoons chopped fresh dill

3 teaspoons powdered gelatine

3 tablespoons dry white wine

2 eggs, separated

3 heaped tablespoons finely shredded

lettuce

to garnish:

extra shredded lettuce

8 cooked, unpeeled prawns

1 Grease four individual moulds, about 150–200 ml/¼–⅓ pint capacity.
2 Put the prawns and fish stock into a liquidizer or food processor and blend until smooth. Blend in the yogurt and dill.
3 Put the gelatine and wine into a small bowl and set aside for 1 minute. Stand the bowl in a pan of hot water and leave until the gelatine has dissolved, about 2 minutes.
4 Beat the egg yolks into the fish and yogurt mixture and add the dissolved gelatine; leave in a cool place until the mixture just starts to set. Whisk the egg whites until stiff but not dry, and fold lightly but thoroughly into the setting mixture, together with the lettuce.
5 Spoon into the prepared moulds, smoothing the surfaces level.
6 Chill for 3–4 hours until set.
7 Make a bed of lettuce on four small plates; carefully unmould a set mousse into the centre of each one.
8 Arrange a little lettuce on the top of each serving and garnish with one or two prawns.

Cook's Tip If you do not have moulds of the right size, small tea cups can be used instead.
Variation Instead of shredded lettuce, use shredded, seeded cucumber which has been gently wrung out in a clean cloth to remove the excess moisture.

AUBERGINE AND OLIVE PATE

preparation: 25 minutes

cooking: about 8 minutes

serves 4

2 medium aubergines

2 garlic cloves, peeled and crushed

2 tablespoons chopped coriander

juice of ½ lemon

3 tablespoons olive oil

salt and freshly ground black pepper

10 black olives, stoned and finely chopped

to garnish:

wedges of lemon or lime

1 Put the aubergines onto the rack of the grill pan; 'toast' under a moderately hot grill until the skins start to blacken and blister. Turn the aubergines and continue grilling until the aubergine skins are evenly charred.
2 Either rub off the skins, or halve the aubergines and scoop the flesh into a bowl; mash the aubergine flesh with the garlic, half the coriander, the lemon juice, olive oil, and salt and pepper to taste. Alternatively this can be done in a liquidizer or food processor, for a smoother result.
3 Mix in the olives. Spoon onto individual plates and sprinkle with the remaining chopped coriander.
4 Garnish with wedges of lemon or lime and serve with wholemeal toast or warm wholemeal pitta bread.

Cook's Tip If you want to make the pâté go further, or if you want to reduce the strength of the flavour, mix in a little homemade yogurt (page 139).
Variation Substitute the mashed flesh of one small avocado for the flesh of one of the charred aubergines.

RICOTTA AND BASIL MOUSSE

preparation: 25 minutes, plus chilling

serves 4

•

225 g/8 oz Ricotta cheese

150 ml/¼ pint homemade yogurt
(page 139)

5 tablespoons chicken stock (page 137)

1 garlic clove, peeled

1 tablespoon chopped basil

2 tablespoons pine kernels, chopped

salt and freshly ground black pepper

3 teaspoons powdered gelatine

2 tablespoons water

1 teaspoon green peppercorns

12 basil leaves

1 Grease and line a 450 g/1 lb loaf tin or terrine with non-stick silicone or greased greaseproof paper.
2 Put the Ricotta cheese, yogurt, stock, garlic and chopped basil into a liquidizer or food processor; blend until smooth.
3 Mix in the pine kernels and add salt and pepper to taste.
4 Put the gelatine and water into a small bowl and set aside for 1 minute. Stand in a pan of hot water and leave until the gelatine has dissolved, about 2 minutes. Stir the dissolved gelatine into the cheese mixture. Leave on one side for a few minutes until it starts to thicken.
5 Stir the green peppercorns into the mousse mixture.
6 Spoon half the mixture into the prepared loaf tin or terrine and lay the basil leaves over the top; add the remaining mousse mixture, spreading the surface level with a knife.
7 Chill for 4 hours or until firm enough to slice.
8 Turn the mousse out and serve cut into slices, on individual plates, with each slice of mousse sitting in a little Tomato Sauce (page 138).

Cook's Tip After the gelatine has been added to the mousse mixture, it can be put into the freezer for a minute or two, in order to thicken it more quickly.
Variation Watercress can be used in place of basil; use 2 tablespoons coarsely chopped watercress in the mousse mixture, and lay several large watercress leaves through the middle of the mousse.

CHEESE AND HERB ROULADE

preparation: 25 minutes

cooking: about 25 minutes

oven temperature: 190°C, 375°F, Gas Mark 5

serves 4–6

•

25 g/1 oz butter

25 g/1 oz wholemeal flour

150 ml/¼ pint skimmed milk

225 g/8 oz curd cheese

2 tablespoons grated Parmesan cheese

salt and freshly ground black pepper

1 tablespoon chopped tarragon

1 tablespoon chopped basil

3 eggs, separated

filling:

3 tablespoons fromage blanc (page 140)

1 tablespoon chopped herbs

1 garlic clove, peeled and crushed

salt and freshly ground black pepper

topping:

2 tablespoons grated Parmesan cheese

1 Grease a Swiss roll tin (about 30 × 20 cm/12 × 8 inch), and line it with non-stick silicone paper or greased greaseproof paper.
2 Melt the butter in a pan; stir in the flour and cook for 30 seconds. Gradually stir in the milk, and cook gently until the sauce has thickened.
3 Remove from the heat and beat in the curd cheese, Parmesan cheese, salt and pepper to taste, tarragon, basil and egg yolks.
4 Beat the egg whites until stiff but not dry; fold lightly but thoroughly into the herb sauce. Spread evenly into the lined tin.
5 Bake in the preheated oven for about 18 minutes until set but still spongy to the touch.
6 Turn onto a fresh sheet of non-stick silicone paper or greased greaseproof paper, which has been laid on top of a clean teatowel. Quickly make the filling by mixing the fromage blanc with the chopped herbs, garlic, and salt and pepper to taste.
7 Remove the lining paper from the roulade. Spread the flavoured fromage blanc over the top and roll up like a Swiss roll, so that it is neatly enclosed in the fresh sheet of non-stick silicone paper and the teatowel.
8 Carefully remove the teatowel and non-stick silicone paper and place the assembled roulade on a shallow ovenproof serving dish; sprinkle with the grated Parmesan cheese. Return to the oven for 3–4 minutes.
9 Serve immediately, cut into slices, either on its own or with Tomato Sauce (page 138).

Cook's Tip It is important to line the tin very carefully so that the cooked roulade is a neat shape; if the paper is not pushed well into the corners, the cooked roulade will be irregular in shape.
Variation Instead of adding the curd cheese to the roulade mixture, you can add 225 g/8 oz finely puréed green vegetable, such as spinach or broccoli. Make sure that it is well drained before adding to the mixture.

MINIATURE STUFFED VEGETABLES

preparation: 30 minutes

serves 4

•

8 button tomatoes

8 small courgettes, topped and tailed

8 button mushrooms, with unblemished skins

1½ tablespoons tapenade (see Cook's Tip)

3 tablespoons hummus (page 25)

2 tablespoons taramasalata

to garnish:

oak leaf lettuce or endive

chopped herbs or paprika (optional)

1 Cut a thin slice from the stalk end of each tomato; carefully hollow out the centre with a coffee spoon. Turn upside down to drain on paper towels.
2 Using a canelle cutter, cut lengthways ridges at regular intervals along each courgette; using a sharp knife, cut a thin lengthways slice from each one and carefully hollow out the centre.
3 Twist off the stalks from the mushrooms, taking care not to break the 'cups'.
4 Spoon a little tapenade into each hollowed tomato; fill the hollowed courgettes with the hummus; fill the mushroom cups with the taramasalata.
5 Arrange all the filled vegetables on a flat serving platter and garnish with small pieces of oak leaf lettuce or endive. The vegetables can be sprinkled with chopped herbs or a little paprika, if liked.

Cook's Tip Tapenade can be bought ready made in a jar; if you would prefer to make your own, use the recipe on page 25. It keeps in a screw-topped jar in the refrigerator for up to 2 weeks.
All the vegetable trimmings can be used for a soup.
Variation A well-flavoured fish pâté or the Aubergine and Olive Pâté (page 20) could be used as alternative fillings. A little oil and vinegar dressing can be sprinkled over the vegetables just before serving, for those who would prefer to soften the 'crunch' of the vegetables.

LETTUCE AND VEGETABLE PARCELS

preparation: 25 minutes

cooking: 3 minutes

serves 4

•

4 medium courgettes, topped, tailed and shredded

3 large carrots, peeled and shredded

1 leek, split, cleaned and shredded

225 g/8 oz hummus (page 25)

salt and freshly ground black pepper

1 tablespoon chopped parsley

8 medium-to-large lettuce leaves (use a variety of lettuce that is quite pliable)

2 teaspoons pesto sauce

3 tablespoons chicken stock (page 137)

1 tablespoon olive oil

1 Blanch the vegetables in boiling water for about 1 minute; drain thoroughly and refresh quickly in cold water. Drain very thoroughly on paper towels.
2 Mix the blanched vegetables with the hummus, and salt and pepper to taste; stir in the parsley.
3 Blanch the lettuce leaves in boiling water for 30−60 seconds; remove and drain immediately on paper towels.
4 Divide the vegetable and hummus mixture between four of the lettuce leaves, and pull the lettuce edges up and over the filling. Cover each one with a second blanched lettuce leaf and carefully wrap to completely enclose the filling and make four neat parcels.
5 Place one on each small serving plate. Mix the pesto sauce with the stock and olive oil and trickle a little over each lettuce and vegetable parcel.

Cook's Tip Cabbage, or round, lettuce is the best one to use; the really crisp varieties are almost impossible to shape. The prepared shredded vegetables in brine sold in jars are excellent and do save time. Rinse and drain the vegetables well before using.
Variation To give the parcels a delicate flavour of fish, use taramasalata in place of hummus.

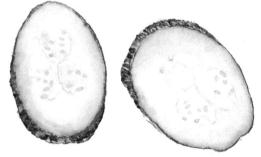

Miniature Stuffed Vegetables: *Baby courgettes, button mushrooms
and cherry tomatoes serve as edible containers for three delicious fillings –
taramasalata, hummus and tapenade.*

TOMATO AND BASIL SORBET

preparation: 10 minutes, plus freezing

serves 4

550 g/1¼ lb tomatoes, skinned and
chopped

300 ml/½ pint chicken stock (page 137)

½ teaspoon brown sugar

1½ tablespoons chopped basil

1 garlic clove, peeled

salt and freshly ground black pepper

3 tablespoons crème fraîche

to garnish:

sprigs of fresh basil

1 Put the tomatoes into a liquidizer or food processor with the stock, sugar, basil, garlic, and salt and pepper to taste; blend until smooth.
2 Press the tomato mixture through a sieve; beat in the crème fraîche until well mixed.
3 Pour into a shallow container and freeze for 3−4 hours, until a firm slush is formed − it should not be solid ice, but just crystalline.
4 Scoop into tall stemmed glasses, garnish each portion with a sprig of fresh basil, and serve immediately.

Cook's Tip If the sorbet has been left in the freezer too long and becomes too firm, leave it at room temperature for about 30 minutes, and break it up gently into ice crystals before serving; but take care not to allow it to melt completely.

Variation This sorbet has a very subtle flavour; for a stronger-flavoured sorbet in which tomato is less dominant, you can use canned consommé instead of the chicken stock.

ARTICHOKES TARTARE

preparation: 25 minutes

cooking: 20−30 minutes

serves 4

4 plump globe artichokes

½ lemon

sauce:

2 tablespoons crème fraîche

4 tablespoons homemade yogurt
(page 139)

½ teaspoon French mustard

1 tablespoon finely chopped gherkin

1 tablespoon capers, chopped

1 garlic clove, peeled and crushed

salt and freshly ground black pepper

2 tablespoons finely chopped parsley

1 Cut off the stem from each artichoke, trimming it level with the base.
2 Cut a thin slice (about 2 cm/¾ inch thick) from the pointed top of each artichoke, with a very sharp knife, to give a flat surface.
3 Brush the cut surfaces with the lemon to prevent discoloration. (If the tip of each leaf is also trimmed, this tends to detract from the overall appearance.)
4 Lower the artichokes into a large pan of boiling water; bring back to the boil and cook until just tender − about 20−30 minutes, but the time will depend on the size and age of the artichokes. (If you pull at a base leaf, it should come away easily.)
5 Meanwhile prepare the sauce: mix the crème fraîche with the yogurt, mustard, gherkin, capers, garlic, salt and pepper to taste and the parsley.
6 Lift the cooked artichokes out of the pan with a slotted spoon and drain upside-down for a few moments on several thicknesses of paper towels.
7 Place a warm artichoke the right way up on individual serving plates and provide each person with a small bowl of sauce for dunking the base of the leaves.

Cook's Tip Remember to remind guests about the inedible 'hairy choke' which lies under the centre leaves, at the base of the artichoke. It hides the delicious artichoke heart, which is the most succulent part. Once you have eaten the centre leaves, it is quite easy to cut out the choke and the heart can then be cut into small pieces and dipped into the sauce. Do provide finger bowls, as globe artichokes are very messy to eat.

Variation As an alternative presentation, you can lift out the centre leaves carefully by twisting, so that they come out like a bud, and put beside each cooked artichoke on its serving plate. Remove the chokes carefully and spoon some sauce into the cavity of each artichoke.

HUMMUS

preparation: 10 minutes, plus soaking

cooking: 1 hour

serves 4

150 g/5 oz dried chick peas, soaked in cold
water overnight

chicken stock (page 137)

3 tablespoons olive oil

150 ml/¼ pint homemade yogurt (page 139)

2 garlic cloves, peeled

juice of 1 lemon

salt and freshly ground black pepper

1 Drain the chick peas and put them into a pan with sufficient stock to cover well; bring to the boil and simmer, covered, for about 1 hour until just tender. Drain them thoroughly.

2 Put the cooked chick peas into a liquidizer or food processor, together with the olive oil, yogurt, garlic, and lemon juice; blend until smooth. If you want the hummus to be a little thinner, blend in a little extra chicken stock.

3 Add salt and pepper to taste and serve with warm wholemeal pitta bread.

Cook's Tip For speed, use 1 × 425g/15 oz can chick peas, rinsed and drained, instead; you then eliminate the soaking and fairly lengthy cooking times.

Variation If you add sufficient chicken stock to give the hummus a pouring consistency, it makes a delicious sauce for cooked pasta. Heat through gently and add some chopped coriander or parsley.

CRUDITES WITH TAPENADE

preparation: 10 minutes, plus chilling

serves 4

2 large carrots, peeled and cut into thin
sticks

½ cucumber, halved lengthways, seeded
and cut into thin sticks

2 celery sticks, cut into thin sticks

1 large red pepper, cored, seeded and cut
into thin sticks

8 button mushrooms

tapenade:

75g/3 oz stoned black olives

3 anchovy fillets

1 tablespoon capers

3 tablespoons olive oil

1 tablespoon brandy

1 garlic clove, peeled

2 teaspoons lemon juice

3 tablespoons thick homemade yogurt
(page 139)

freshly ground black pepper

1 To make the tapenade, put the olives, anchovy fillets, capers, olive oil, brandy, garlic, and lemon juice into a liquidizer or food processor; blend until smooth.

2 Mix the tapenade with the yogurt and add pepper to taste.

3 Put into a bowl, cover with cling film and chill for 1 hour.

4 Serve with a selection of the prepared vegetables as dunks.

Cook's Tip To ensure that the vegetable crudités are really crisp, soak them in a bowl of iced water for 30 minutes before serving and then drain them thoroughly.

Variation Halve hard-boiled eggs lengthways and carefully scoop out the yolks; mash the yolks with some of the tapenade to make a smooth paste and mound back into the halves of egg white. Garnish with extra capers and anchovy fillets.

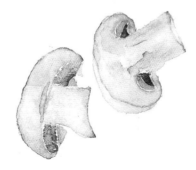

Salads

To some people, a salad is still merely lettuce, cucumber and tomato; to others, a salad is a dish in its own right, full of colour and texture, and enhanced by a subtle dressing.

As there is now such an enormous choice of ingredients widely available throughout the year, you can let your imagination run riot when preparing a salad. For example, there are many varieties of lettuce, apart from the round cabbage lettuce (sometimes rather disparagingly called English lettuce) and the familiar long-leafed cos. The very crisp iceberg is just as compact as white cabbage. Radicchio is a cross between a red lettuce and a small cabbage; the ridged leaves are tightly packed and are a deep purplish-pink. Continental, or oak leaf, lettuce has curly leaves which are shaded from dark green to deep purple and look extremely pretty.

Other 'salad greens' include curly endive; lamb's lettuce, which looks like small green tongues; and sorrel, which is similar to a small-leafed spinach. You can also use more traditional ingredients such as chicory, watercress, tomatoes and spring onions.

With all the salads in this chapter, the dressing complements the other ingredients, marrying all the flavours together. It is important that none should dominate. My *Lean Cuisine* dressings are not the traditional high-calorie vinaigrette: some are based on pure fruit juices, others use fish stock and white wine (for fish salads) and there is a very good low-calorie 'mayonnaise' based on homemade yogurt. All the delicious dressings used in this chapter are 'lean' and low in fat.

Some of the salads in this section are healthier versions of classics such as Caesar Salad, while others have one or more unusual but delicious ingredients . . . take nasturtiums, for example. A warm salad, or *salade tiede*, such as Warm Potato Salad with Thyme, is guaranteed to win over the least enthusiastic of salad eaters with its crisp combination of fresh salad ingredients, lightly cooked vegetables and special hot dressing.

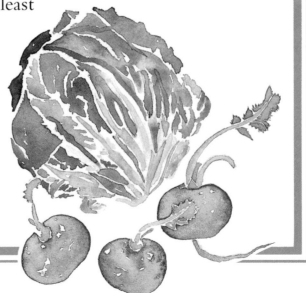

MUSSEL AND RADICCHIO SALAD

preparation: 25 minutes

cooking: 5 minutes

serves 4

32 fresh mussels

300 ml/½ pint dry white wine

2 garlic cloves, peeled and finely chopped

2 tablespoons coarsely chopped parsley

1 small onion, peeled and thinly sliced

salt and freshly ground black pepper

2 egg yolks

½ teaspoon French mustard

1 tablespoon chopped tarragon

2 chicory heads, shredded

2 radicchio heads, cut into thin wedges

to garnish:

sprigs of fresh basil

few cooked mussels in shells (optional)

1 Scrub the mussels thoroughly and make sure that none of them has damaged shells.

2 Put the mussels into a pan with the white wine, garlic, parsley, onion, and salt and pepper to taste; cover the pan and cook for 5 minutes, shaking the pan from time to time, until the shells open. If any mussels stay firmly shut, discard them.

3 Remove the mussels from their shells and strain the cooking liquid.

4 Measure off 150 ml/¼ pint of the mussel cooking liquid and beat with the egg yolks, mustard, salt and pepper to taste, and the tarragon.

5 Arrange the chicory and radicchio on four small plates. Put the shelled mussels on top and spoon over the prepared dressing.

6 Garnish with sprigs of fresh basil, and a few extra cooked mussels in their shells, if liked.

Cook's Tip The easiest way to clean mussels is to scrub them with a stiff nail brush under cold running water.

The overall flavour is better if you prepare this salad quite quickly, so that the mussels and the dressing are still slightly warm.

If you are using cooked mussels in their shells as a garnish, brush the shells with a little olive oil to give them a really good shine.

Variation Large peeled Mediterranean prawns can be used in this salad, instead of shelled mussels. Add a little lemon juice or rind to the dressing.

WARM CHEESE SALAD

preparation: 25 minutes

cooking: 4–5 minutes

serves 4

175 g/6 oz mangetout

175 g/6 oz haricots verts

Continental red, or oak leaf, lettuce

4 tablespoons olive oil

2 tablespoons white wine vinegar

salt and freshly ground black pepper

2 tablespoons blanched almonds, toasted and finely chopped

12 small thin slices wholemeal French bread

3 teaspoons pesto sauce

100 g/4 oz goat cheese, crumbled

to garnish:

1 tablespoon toasted almonds, chopped

1 Cook the mangetout and the haricots verts in boiling water, in separate pans, for just 3 minutes. (If the haricots verts are quite large, allow a minute or so longer; if the mangetout are quite small, reduce the cooking time.) Drain the vegetables thoroughly and refresh both in really cold water. Drain again thoroughly.

2 Arrange a bed of Continental red, or oak leaf, lettuce on four small plates; arrange the mangetout and haricots verts decoratively on top.

3 Mix the olive oil with the white wine vinegar, salt and pepper to taste, and the almonds.

4 Toast the slices of wholemeal French bread lightly on one side and turn them over, mix the pesto sauce and goat cheese together and spread over the untoasted sides.

5 Toast the cheese-topped croûtes until pale golden and puffy; arrange on top of each salad and immediately spoon over the dressing.

6 Garnish with the almonds, and serve immediately.

Cook's Tip If goat cheese is difficult to buy, curd cheese can be used instead; add a squeeze of lemon juice to give it a similar tangy flavour. The vegetables look more attractive if they are not 'topped and tailed'; but this is a matter of personal preference.

Variation Instead of spreading the small croûtes of bread with goat cheese, try spreading them with pâté and a sprinkling of grated Parmesan cheese. Put under the grill for a minute or two, as above.

Warm Cheese Salad: *A wonderful contrast in flavours and textures.*
Mussel and Radicchio Salad: *A colourful combination of fresh mussels
and radicchio.*

WARM POTATO SALAD WITH THYME

preparation: 10 minutes

cooking: 10 minutes

serves 4

550 g/1¼ lb new potatoes, washed and scrubbed but not peeled

salt and freshly ground black pepper

sprig of mint (optional)

grated rind and juice of 1 lemon

½ teaspoon soft brown sugar

3 spring onions, topped, tailed and finely chopped

3 tablespoons olive oil

1 tablespoon chopped thyme

1 garlic clove, peeled and crushed

1 Cook the new potatoes in boiling salted water until just tender — about 8–10 minutes. Cook with mint for extra flavour.
2 Meanwhile put the lemon rind and juice, brown sugar, spring onions, olive oil, thyme and garlic into a shallow pan, and heat through until the mixture is just bubbling. Season to taste with salt and pepper.
3 Drain the cooked new potatoes thoroughly and toss immediately in the prepared dressing.
4 Leave to stand for 4–5 minutes to give the potatoes the chance to absorb the flavour of the dressing, and then serve while still warm.

Cook's Tip If you do not have any fresh mint, then ½ teaspoon concentrated mint sauce can be added to the cooking water instead.
Variation Add 100 g/4 oz finely chopped lean ham to the dressing before pouring it over the potatoes.

MUSHROOM AND BLUE CHEESE SALAD

preparation: 15 minutes

serves 4

225 g/8 oz firm white button mushrooms, very thinly sliced

1 tablespoon chopped chives

75 g/3 oz Dolcelatte cheese

3 tablespoons homemade yogurt (page 139)

1 teaspoon pesto sauce

salt and freshly ground pepper

1 tablespoon grated Parmesan cheese

1 Put the mushrooms into a bowl with the chives.
2 Put the Dolcelatte cheese into a liquidizer or food processor with the yogurt, pesto sauce, and salt and pepper to taste; blend until smooth.
3 Stir the dressing into the mushrooms, taking care not to spoil their shape.
4 Sprinkle the Parmesan cheese over the salad.

Cook's Tip This makes a delicious accompaniment to lean roast beef instead of creamed horseradish; it is also very good as a side salad with grilled fish or chicken.
Variation Sprinkle with lightly toasted pine kernels instead of the grated Parmesan cheese.

COURGETTE AND ANCHOVY SALAD

preparation: 10 minutes

serves 4

450 g/1 lb firm courgettes, topped and tailed

4 spring onions, topped, tailed and finely chopped

3 tablespoons olive oil

2 tablespoons lemon juice

1 garlic clove, peeled and crushed

4 anchovy fillets, finely chopped

2 teaspoons capers

salt and freshly ground black pepper

to garnish:

4 anchovy fillets, cut in half lengthways

1 Put the courgettes through the shredder blade of a food processor to make long spiral threads. Alternatively, grate them coarsely. Mix with the spring onions.
2 Mix the olive oil with the lemon juice, garlic, anchovy fillets, capers, and salt and pepper to taste.
3 Stir the dressing into the salad so that the courgettes are evenly coated.
4 Arrange the anchovy fillet strips decoratively on the top.

Cook's Tip If you do not have either a food processor or a grater with a coarse cutting surface, cut the courgettes into matchstick strips by hand.
Variation Try using equal quantities of courgettes and carrots; the colour contrast is very effective.

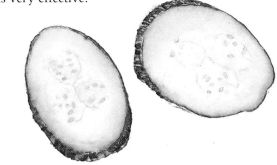

CAESAR SALAD

preparation: 15 minutes

cooking: 1 minute

serves 4

1 cos lettuce, torn into shreds

few sprigs of watercress

3 tablespoons olive oil

4 anchovy fillets, chopped

1 tablespoon lemon juice

1 teaspoon French mustard

2 teaspoons Worcestershire sauce

2 garlic cloves, peeled and crushed

salt and freshly ground black pepper

2 eggs

6 Dry-bake Herb Croûtons (page 140)

1 Place the lettuce in a large salad bowl with the watercress.
2 Mix the olive oil with the anchovy fillets, lemon juice, French mustard, Worcestershire sauce, garlic, and salt and pepper to taste.
3 Put the eggs into a pan with just enough cold water to cover; bring quickly to the boil, cooking for a total of 1 minute.
4 Crack the eggs carefully over the jug of dressing and scoop out the contents of the shells. Beat into the dressing.
5 Pour the dressing over the salad; break in the croûtons and toss together.
6 Serve immediately.

Cook's Tip These eggs are hardly cooked at all; if you are worried that people will not like the taste of semi-raw egg white, cook them for a little longer.
Variation Try mixing different varieties of lettuce together, such as cos, radicchio and oak leaf.

SIMPLE SEAFOOD SALAD

preparation: 35 minutes

cooking: 15–20 minutes

serves 4

350 g/12 oz fresh squid, skinned and cleaned

juice of ½ lemon

300 ml/½ pint fish stock (page 137)

2 tablespoons chopped parsley

salt and freshly ground black pepper

600 ml/1 pint fresh mussels

2 garlic cloves, peeled and finely chopped

1 tablespoon chopped dill

300 ml/½ pint dry white wine

8 Mediterranean prawns

100 g/4 oz cooked cockles

4 tablespoons olive oil

juice of 1 lemon

samphire (see Variation)

pieces of curly endive

1 Your fishmonger should be willing to clean and partially prepare the squid for you; it can be very messy. Make sure that the 'tubes' of squid are thoroughly clean and cut them into rings about 5 mm/¼ inch thick.

2 Put the rings of squid and the tentacles into a shallow pan with the lemon juice, fish stock, parsley, and salt and pepper to taste; cook gently in a covered pan for 10 minutes until the squid is just tender.

3 Meanwhile, scrub the mussels, making sure that none of them has broken shells. Put the mussels into a pan with the garlic, dill, white wine, and salt and pepper to taste. Cover and cook for 5 minutes, shaking the pan from time to time, until the shells open. If any mussels stay firmly shut, discard them.

4 Drain the rings and tentacles of cooked squid, discarding the cooking liquid; remove the cooked mussels, reserving their cooking liquid. Shell some of the mussels and leave the remainder in their shells.

5 Remove the heads neatly from the Mediterranean prawns, leaving the body shells and tails intact.

6 Mix the cooked squid with the shelled mussels, Mediterranean prawns and cockles.

7 Mix the olive oil with the lemon juice, 5 tablespoons of the strained mussel cooking liquid, and salt and pepper to taste. Stir the dressing into the shellfish.

8 Arrange a bed of samphire on each of four small plates, and spoon the prepared seafood salad on top.

9 Garnish with the unshelled mussels, and tuck a few pieces of curly endive in between the different shellfish.

Cook's Tip Save any remaining liquid from cooking the squid and the mussels and use as the base for a fish soup, making it up to the desired amount with water or dry white wine.

Variation Samphire is a very fine seaweed, with a fresh salty flavour; it can be bought from many good fishmongers. If you cannot find it, use young fresh spinach leaves or simply garnish with young blanched vine leaves.

CARROT AND WALNUT SALAD

preparation: 15 minutes

serves 4

450 g/1 lb large carrots, peeled

1 small onion, peeled and thinly sliced

grated rind and juice of 1 orange

juice of ½ lemon

3 tablespoons olive oil

1 garlic clove, peeled

75 g/3 oz walnuts, roughly chopped

salt and freshly ground black pepper

50 g/2 oz sultanas

to garnish:

2 tablespoons chopped parsley

1 Either put the carrots through the shredder blade of a food processor, or grate them coarsely. Mix in a bowl with the thinly sliced onion.

2 Put the orange rind and juice, lemon juice, olive oil, garlic and 50 g/2 oz of the walnuts into a liquidizer or food processor; blend until smooth. Add salt and pepper to taste.

3 Stir the prepared dressing into the carrot mixture, together with the remaining walnuts and the sultanas. Sprinkle with parsley.

Cook's Tip Carrots discolour very quickly once peeled; if you are not going to complete the salad straight away, stir some of the orange or lemon juice into the shredded carrot, and keep it covered with cling film.

Variation Try using equal quantities of grated carrot and grated parsnip; the flavour of both is slightly sweet and they blend very well together. Use hazelnuts instead of walnuts.

Simple Seafood Salad: *A selection of poached shellfish attractively garnished with young vine leaves and curly endive, moistened with a light fishy dressing.*

BROWN RICE AND MIXED HERB SALAD

preparation: 10 minutes, plus chilling

cooking: 30—35 minutes

serves 4

1 small onion, peeled and finely chopped

4 tablespoons olive oil

1 garlic clove, peeled and finely chopped

½ teaspoon garam masala

150 g/5 oz long-grain brown rice

pinch of powdered saffron

400 ml/14 fl oz chicken stock (page 137)

1 tablespoon desiccated coconut

salt and freshly ground black pepper

2 tablespoons tarragon vinegar

1 tablespoon chopped coriander

2 tablespoons chopped parsley

2 tablespoons cashew nuts, toasted

1 Fry the onion gently in 1 tablespoon of the olive oil for 3 minutes; add the garlic, garam masala and rice, and fry gently for a further 2 minutes, stirring continuously.

2 Stir in the saffron, chicken stock, desiccated coconut, and salt and pepper to taste; bring to the boil and simmer gently for about 25 minutes, until the rice is just tender.

3 Mix the remaining olive oil with the tarragon vinegar, salt and pepper to taste, and the coriander and parsley; stir evenly through the warm rice, together with the cashew nuts.

4 Allow to cool before serving.

Cook's Tip The quality of brown rice varies enormously, and some types absorb more liquid while cooking than others; check from time to time to see that the rice is not becoming too dry, and if necessary add extra chicken stock.

Variation To turn this very basic rice salad into a more colourful dish, add chopped red and green peppers, coarsely grated carrot and seeded and diced cucumber.

BROAD BEAN AND ORANGE SALAD

preparation: 30 minutes, plus chilling

serves 4

1k/2 lb young broad beans, unshelled weight

3 large oranges

3 tablespoons olive oil

1 garlic clove, peeled and crushed

salt and freshly ground black pepper

1 teaspoon chopped thyme

75 g/3 oz Mozzarella cheese, cut into small cubes

1 Shell the broad beans into a bowl.

2 Grate the rind and squeeze the juice from one of the oranges; remove all the peel and pith from the remaining oranges and cut into neat segments. Add the segments to the broad beans.

3 Mix the orange rind and juice with the olive oil, garlic, salt and pepper to taste, and the thyme.

4 Stir the dressing into the beans and orange segments, together with the Mozzarella.

5 Chill for about 30 minutes before serving, to allow the flavours to mingle.

Cook's Tip Do not choose pods that are too slim, as you will find the beans are very underdeveloped and hardly worth using.

Variation Instead of shelled broad beans, use very small, topped and tailed mangetout; they can be blanched quickly beforehand if preferred.

MEDITERRANEAN VEGETABLE SALAD

preparation: 5 minutes, plus chilling

cooking: 10 minutes

serves 4

150 ml/¼ pint chicken stock (page 137)

3 tablespoons olive oil

grated rind and juice of 1 orange

2 garlic cloves, peeled and finely chopped

1 small onion, peeled and thinly sliced

sprig of thyme

2 bay leaves

1 tablespoon tomato paste

75 g/3 oz tiny button mushrooms

4 small courgettes, topped, tailed and cut into 2.5 cm/1 inch chunks

1 medium red pepper, cored, seeded and cut into 2.5 cm/1 inch chunks

100 g/4 oz broad beans (shelled weight)

salt and freshly ground black pepper

1 Put the chicken stock into a large frying pan with the olive oil, orange rind and juice, garlic, onion, thyme and bay leaves; simmer for 5 minutes.
2 Stir in the tomato paste until dissolved and then add the prepared vegetables; cover and simmer gently for just 5 minutes. Add salt and pepper to taste and leave to cool.
3 Chill, covered, for 1 hour.
4 Serve with crusty wholemeal bread. (This salad is rather similar in flavour to a ratatouille.)

Cook's Tip The vegetables should still have a 'bite' to them, so make sure that they are not overcooked.
Variation Cubes of aubergine, small trimmed French beans and small artichoke hearts can be used in place of some of the vegetables suggested above.

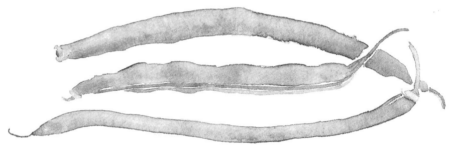

ARTICHOKE HEART AND AVOCADO SALAD

preparation: 15−20 minutes

serves 4

2 × 425 g/15 oz cans artichoke hearts, drained

1 large ripe avocado, halved, stoned and peeled

juice of 1 lemon

finely grated rind of ½ lemon

2 tablespoons olive oil

2 tablespoons orange juice

salt and freshly ground black pepper

1 tablespoon chopped tarragon

1 tablespoon flaked or chopped hazelnuts

1 Cut the artichoke hearts neatly into halves or quarters, depending on their size.
2 Arrange the artichoke hearts on a salad platter.
3 Cut the avocado into thin slivers and toss in lemon juice; then arrange on top of the artichoke hearts.
4 Mix the lemon rind with the olive oil, orange juice, salt and pepper to taste, and the tarragon.
5 Spoon the dressing evenly over the salad and sprinkle with the hazelnuts before serving.

Cook's Tip If you peel the avocado with a swivel potato peeler, it will not remove too much of the deep green flesh just beneath the skin.
Variation Cooked asparagus tips make an excellent alternative to artichoke hearts; use freshly cooked tips when they are in season, or well-drained canned ones.

ENDIVE AND NASTURTIUM SALAD

preparation: 25–30 minutes

serves 4

2 large oranges

1 curly endive head, divided into pieces

½ cucumber, thinly sliced

a handful of nasturtium flowers

3 tablespoons olive oil

juice of 1 orange

salt and freshly ground black pepper

1 tablespoon chopped chives

1 Remove the peel from 1 orange in thin strips, leaving as much pith on the orange as possible. Cut the strips of peel into matchstick strips; place in a small bowl of cold water.

2 Remove all the pith and remaining peel from both oranges; cut into neat segments.

3 Arrange pieces of endive decoratively in a shallow bowl with the cucumber and orange segments. Scatter the nasturtium flowers over the top.

4 Mix the olive oil with the orange juice, salt and pepper to taste and the chives. Spoon the prepared dressing evenly over the salad.

5 Drain the matchstick strips of orange peel and scatter over the top of the salad. Serve immediately.

Cook's Tip Make sure that the nasturtium heads are scrupulously clean before you use them. It is advisable not to experiment with other flowers, unless you know they are safe to eat.

The easiest way to remove the orange peel in thin strips is to use a swivel potato peeler; if the oranges are chilled briefly beforehand, the job is made even simpler.

Variation To turn this salad into a main meal salad for three people, add about 225 g/8 oz of thin strips of cooked chicken or turkey.

LETTUCE HEARTS WITH WATERCRESS MOUSSELINE

preparation: 15–20 minutes

serves 4

hearts from 2 cos lettuces

150 ml/¼ pint homemade yogurt (page 139)

2 garlic cloves, peeled

1 tablespoon white wine vinegar

1 teaspoon honey

1 bunch watercress, washed, trimmed and stalks discarded

2 spring onions, topped, tailed and chopped

salt and freshly ground black pepper

to garnish:

1 tablespoon green pumpkin seeds

1 Quarter each lettuce heart and arrange on a shallow oval dish.

2 Put the yogurt, garlic, white wine vinegar, honey, watercress, spring onions, and salt and pepper to taste into a liquidizer or food processor; blend until smooth. If the mousseline is too thick for your liking at this stage, thin it down with a little skimmed milk.

3 Spoon some of the watercress mousseline over the lettuce hearts and serve the remainder separately.

4 Sprinkle with the pumpkin seeds and serve immediately.

Cook's Tip If you do not have a liquidizer or food processor, chop the watercress leaves very finely before mixing with the other ingredients.

Variation Other lettuce hearts can be used in place of cos provided they are crisp and will not wilt under the dressing; round lettuce is not suitable. Radicchio adds a pretty colour contrast. The dressing is also particularly good spooned over lightly cooked cauliflower florets.

Endive and Nasturtium Salad: *A stunning salad that looks as if it has come fresh from the garden; pretty nasturtium blooms are scattered over the greenery before serving.*

CHICK PEA SALAD WITH MINT MOUSSELINE

preparation: 20 minutes, plus soaking and chilling

cooking: 1 hour

serves 4

175 g/6 oz dried chick peas, soaked in cold water overnight

grated rind and juice of 1 lemon

1 tablespoon garlic vinegar

2 garlic cloves, peeled and crushed

salt and freshly ground black pepper

3 tablespoons olive oil

2 tablespoons sesame seeds, toasted

4 spring onions, topped and tailed

2 tablespoons homemade yogurt (page 139)

2 tablespoons Yogurt Mayonnaise (page 139)

1 tablespoon chopped mint

to garnish:

sprigs of fresh mint

1 Drain the chick peas and put them into a pan with sufficient fresh cold water to cover; bring to the boil and simmer, covered, for about 1 hour until tender.
2 Meanwhile prepare the dressing: mix the lemon rind and juice with the garlic vinegar, garlic, salt and pepper to taste, olive oil and the sesame seeds.
3 Drain the chick peas and stir in the dressing while they are still warm. Mix in the chopped spring onions and allow to cool. Chill for 30 minutes.
4 Prepare the mousseline by mixing the yogurt with the Yogurt Mayonnaise and mint.
5 Spoon the chick pea salad onto a serving dish and garnish with sprigs of mint. Pass the mint mousseline separately in a small bowl.

Cook's Tip If you want to cut down on the time spent in the kitchen, use well-rinsed and drained canned chick peas in place of cooked dried ones.
Variation Instead of adding a dressing to the cooked chick peas, stir in some Herb and Lemon Sauce (page 138) and some sliced raw button mushrooms. Serve warm, without the Mint Mousseline.

FRENCH BEAN MIMOSA SALAD

preparation: 20 minutes, plus chilling

cooking: 5 minutes

serves 4

350 g/12 oz French beans

1 garlic clove, peeled and finely chopped

small bunch of parsley stalks

300 ml/½ pint chicken stock (page 137)

salt and freshly ground black pepper

3 tablespoons olive oil

2 tablespoons homemade yogurt (page 139)

1 tablespoon white wine vinegar

3 hard-boiled eggs

1 Cook the French beans in a shallow pan with the garlic, parsley stalks, chicken stock, and salt and pepper to taste for just 5 minutes; remove from the heat, drain the French beans and cool very quickly. Reserve the stock to use for a soup or sauce.
2 Mix the olive oil with the yogurt, wine vinegar, and salt and pepper to taste.
3 Separate the yolks and whites from the hard-boiled eggs; chop the egg whites finely and sieve the yolks.
4 Stir the cooled French beans into the prepared dressing, together with the egg whites.
5 Spoon into a shallow serving dish and sprinkle with the egg yolks.

Cook's Tip French beans look more attractive untrimmed; but if you wish to remove the stalks, the easiest way of doing this is to snip them off with kitchen scissors, holding several beans together at once.
Variation Instead of using chopped and sieved hard-boiled eggs, try adding a 'creamy' scrambled egg to the salad; if you mix the cooked scrambled egg with a little mayonnaise, it keeps its texture very well when served cold.

SPROUTING SALAD

preparation: 10–15 minutes

serves 4

●

50 g/2 oz alfalfa sprouts

50 g/2 oz lentil sprouts

50 g/2 oz mung bean sprouts

50 g/2 oz wheat sprouts

50 g/2 oz plump dried apricots, finely
chopped

25 g/1 oz almonds, chopped (either plain
or lightly toasted)

peeled segments from 2 grapefruit

3 tablespoons grapefruit juice

2 teaspoons honey

2 tablespoons homemade yogurt (page 139)

salt and freshly ground black pepper

1 tablespoon chopped mint

1 Mix all the sprouts lightly together; mix in the apricots, almonds and grapefruit segments.

2 Arrange the mixture on a shallow platter.

3 Mix the grapefruit juice with the honey, yogurt, salt and pepper to taste and the mint.

4 Trickle the dressing evenly over the salad.

Cook's Tip All the sprouts can be obtained from healthfood shops and are usually found in the chilled cabinet with dairy products. You can grow your own sprouting beans very easily, if preferred.

Variation In summer this salad looks very pretty garnished with halved fresh strawberries.

FENNEL SALAD WITH EGG AND CHIVE DRESSING

preparation: 10 minutes

cooking: about 3 minutes

serves 4

●

2 medium fennel heads

3 eggs

1 tablespoon skimmed milk

salt and freshly ground black pepper

1 tablespoon chopped chives

2 tablespoons Yogurt Mayonnaise
(page 139)

1 tablespoon homemade yogurt (page 139)

to garnish:

fresh chives

1 Remove any feathery tops from the fennel and reserve for garnish. Shred the fennel bulbs finely, discarding any discoloured parts.

2 Beat the eggs with the milk, salt and pepper to taste, and the chives; scramble gently in a non-stick pan, until the egg forms soft creamy flakes.

3 Cool the scrambled egg slightly and then stir in the Yogurt Mayonnaise and yogurt.

4 Gently combine the fennel and the cool scrambled egg. Spoon into a serving dish, and top with freshly snipped chives and the feathery sprigs of fennel.

Cook's Tip The easiest way of removing any discoloured parts from the fennel is to use a potato peeler.

Variation To turn this into a main meal, serve the salad on a bed of curly endive and top with some flaked cooked crab or salmon.

CHINESE-STYLE GINGER SALAD

preparation: 15 minutes

serves 4

175 g/6 oz fresh bean sprouts

1 × 225 g/8 oz can water chestnuts, drained and thinly sliced

25 g/1 oz Chinese dried mushrooms, soaked in tepid water for 10 minutes, and thinly sliced

8 shelled lychees, stoned and chopped (fresh or canned)

small piece of fresh root ginger, about 1 cm/½ inch thick, peeled and grated

2 tablespoons fresh pineapple juice

3 tablespoons olive oil

1 garlic clove, peeled and cut into thin strips

1 teaspoon soy sauce

salt and freshly ground black pepper

1 Mix the bean sprouts with the water chestnuts, mushrooms and lychees.

2 Mix the root ginger with the pineapple juice, olive oil, garlic, soy sauce, and salt and pepper to taste.

3 Stir the prepared dressing into the salad and toss together with the ingredients.

Cook's Tip If you find the root ginger difficult to grate, squeeze it through a garlic press instead.

Variation Add some thin strips of cooked chicken to turn this into a main-meal salad.

GRILLED PEPPER SALAD

preparation: 25 minutes, plus chilling

cooking: 6–8 minutes

serves 4

2 large green peppers

2 large red peppers

1 small onion, peeled and chopped

4 tomatoes, skinned, seeded and chopped

2 garlic cloves, peeled and chopped

3 tablespoons olive oil

grated rind and juice of ½ orange

salt and freshly ground black pepper

1 Lay the peppers on the rack of the grill pan; place under a moderately hot grill, making sure that the peppers are not actually touching the element or flame. Cook under the grill for about 8 minutes until the skins blister and char, turning the peppers from time to time.

2 Peel off the charred pepper skins and cut the flesh into strips; put into a shallow serving dish.

3 Put the onion, tomatoes, garlic, olive oil, orange rind and juice, and salt and pepper to taste into a liquidizer or food processor; blend until smooth.

4 Stir the tomato mixture into the prepared pepper strips until these are evenly coated. Cover and chill for 1 hour.

Cook's Tip You may find it easier to regulate the cooking of the peppers by doing it over a gas flame: spike the peppers onto large metal skewers and balance above the gas flame. They will still need to be turned from time to time.

Variation Try using different coloured peppers; many supermarkets and greengrocers now also stock the white and yellow varieties.

SHREDDED BEEF SALAD

preparation: 20 minutes

serves 4

2 medium chicory heads, divided into leaves

8 radishes, thinly sliced

2 medium leeks, split, cleaned and cut into thin strips

225 g/8 oz lean rare roast beef, cut into thin strips

2 tablespoons roughly chopped walnuts

2 teaspoons freshly grated horseradish

1 garlic clove, peeled and crushed

1 tablespoon finely chopped watercress

2 tablespoons homemade yogurt (page 139)

1 tablespoon dry sherry

salt and freshly ground black pepper

to garnish:

sprigs of watercress

1 Arrange the chicory leaves like a fan on a serving dish.
2 Mix the radishes with the strips of leek and add the strips of beef. Arrange on top of the chicory and sprinkle with the walnuts.
3 Mix the horseradish with the garlic, watercress, yogurt, sherry, and salt and pepper to taste.
4 Trickle the dressing over the prepared salad and garnish with watercress.

Cook's Tip If you are cooking the beef yourself, choose a very lean cut, brush it lightly with melted butter or oil, rather than adding knobs of fat, and enclose it in a foil parcel with a little stock or wine for added moisture.
Variation Smoked chicken makes a good substitute for roast beef.

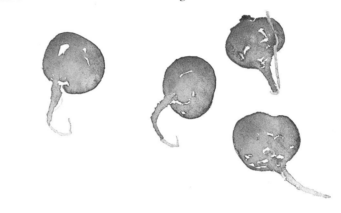

BRUSSELS SPROUT AND STILTON SALAD

preparation: 20 minutes

serves 4

450 g/1 lb firm, well-shaped Brussels sprouts

3 small spring onions, finely chopped

2 tablespoons coarsely chopped walnuts

50 g/2 oz Stilton cheese, coarsely crumbled

dressing:

juice and grated rind ½ orange

1 tablespoon olive oil

2 tablespoons homemade yogurt

1 garlic clove, peeled and crushed

salt and freshly ground black pepper

4 cup-shaped young cabbage leaves

poppy seeds

1   Shred the Brussels sprouts finely, either by hand or using the food processor.
2   Mix the shredded sprouts with the spring onions, walnuts and crumbled cheese.
3   Mix all the dressing ingredients together; stir into the prepared salad ingredients and toss lightly.
4   Place a cabbage leaf on each of four small plates and fill with the prepared salad. Sprinkle with poppy seeds.

Cook's Tip   Make sure that the outer rind has been removed from the Stilton, otherwise it will give the salad a very dry and chalky flavour.
Variation   Shredded Chinese leaves can be used in place of Brussels sprouts.

Vegetables

Vegetables are not just food for vegetarians. They have been sadly neglected by many of us in the past, and, more often than not, badly cooked. Beautifully prepared, perfectly cooked, really fresh vegetables can be the highlight of a meal, irrespective of whether they are served as an accompaniment or as a separate course.

When buying fresh vegetables, choose carefully and remember that most of them are best used within 24 hours of purchase. Store them in a cool, well-ventilated larder or the crisper drawer of a refrigerator until required.

Vegetables retain their maximum flavour when left in their natural state. The secret is to peel and trim only when absolutely necessary. Keep the skins *on* new potatoes; if peas are very young, cook them in their pods (the same applies to broad beans); and do not denude cauliflower of all its greenery.

Cook vegetables carefully and lightly, so that they keep their natural texture, taste, colour and vitamins; it is always preferable to err on the side of undercooking. Most vegetables are best cooked either in a steamer or in a covered pan with the minimum amount of liquid (stock or water). If you do not have a steamer, then you can fit a colander or large sieve over a pan of simmering water and cover it with a lid or piece of foil.

Accompanying vegetables should enhance and complement the fish, meat or poultry that they are served with. If the main course has a sauce, it is better to avoid vegetable dishes that are topped with a sauce. A good way of finishing off simply cooked vegetables is to stir in a little yogurt mayonnaise or fromage blanc and some chopped herbs.

Some of these vegetable dishes are ideal to serve on their own. Asparagus with Orange Sauce, for example, makes both a wonderful starter and a separate vegetable course, and the Warm Vegetable Platter is perfect for serving unaccompanied.

VEGETABLE CURRY

preparation: 25 minutes

cooking: about 35 minutes

serves 4

1 medium onion, peeled and thinly sliced

2 tablespoons olive oil

1 garlic clove, peeled and finely chopped

1 thin slice fresh root ginger, chopped

1 tablespoon curry powder (page 141)

300 ml/½ pint chicken stock (page 137)

300 ml/½ pint coconut milk
(see below)

4 tablespoons chopped cooked spinach

salt and freshly ground black pepper

1 tablespoon chopped coriander

1 small cauliflower, divided into florets

3 medium courgettes, cut into chunks

100 g/4 oz haricots verts

175 g/6 oz broccoli florets

½ cucumber, halved, seeded and chopped

4 tablespoons fresh peas, lightly cooked

3 tablespoons homemade yogurt (page 139)

to garnish:

wedges of lime

sprigs of fresh coriander

1 Fry the onion gently in the olive oil for 4 minutes; add the garlic, ginger and curry powder and fry for a further minute.

2 Add the chicken stock and coconut milk and bring to the boil; add the spinach and simmer gently for 15 minutes.

3 Add salt and pepper to taste, the coriander, cauliflower florets and courgettes; simmer, covered, for 5 minutes.

4 Add the haricots verts and the broccoli florets and simmer, covered, for a further 5 minutes.

5 Stir in the cucumber, peas and yogurt and heat through gently.

6 Serve piping hot, garnished with wedges of lime and sprigs of fresh coriander. Serve with cooked brown rice.

Cook's Tip To make coconut milk, put 4 tablespoons desiccated coconut into a bowl and pour on 300 ml/½ pint boiling water. Leave to stand for 20—30 minutes. Pour through a sieve, pressing on the coconut to extract as much flavour as possible.

Variation Try other green vegetables such as okra (ladies' fingers), shelled broad beans, chopped green pepper or chopped celery. Chopped peeled avocado gives a delicious flavour and texture to this curry; it should be added with the yogurt.

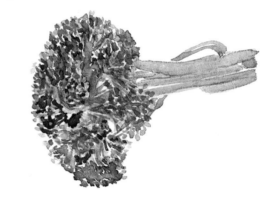

POTATO AND AVOCADO PUREE

preparation: about 10 minutes

cooking: about 15 minutes

serves 4

450 g/1 lb potatoes, peeled and cut into
chunks

sprig of mint

piece of blade mace

1 ripe avocado, halved, stoned and peeled

finely grated rind of ½ lemon

salt and freshly ground black pepper

1 Put the potatoes into a pan with the mint and blade mace; add cold water to cover and bring to the boil. Simmer gently until the potatoes are just tender. Drain thoroughly, discarding the mint and mace.

2 Put the cooked potatoes into a liquidizer or food processor. Add the avocado flesh, lemon rind and salt and pepper to taste; blend until smooth.

3 Heat the purée through gently in a heavy based pan, or in a double saucepan.

Cook's Tip The dish does have a much nuttier flavour if you use small potatoes cooked in their skins.

Variation Stir small cubes of slightly firmer avocado flesh into the prepared warm purée.

Vegetable Curry: *Beautifully cooked green vegetables, still retaining their 'bite', with a mild curry and coconut sauce.*

SPICED PARSNIP PUREE

preparation: 15 minutes

cooking: 10–15 minutes

serves 4

550 g/1¼ lb parsnips, peeled and cut into chunks

small piece of fresh root ginger, bruised

15 g/½ oz butter

2 egg yolks

generous pinch of mixed spice

salt and freshly ground black pepper

1 tablespoon homemade yogurt (page 139)

1 Cook the parsnips in boiling water with the ginger, until just tender. Drain thoroughly.

2 Mash the parsnips and return to a clean saucepan; stir over a gentle heat to dry out the excess moisture.

3 Off the heat, beat in the butter, egg yolks, mixed spice, salt and pepper to taste, and the yogurt. Heat through gently, stirring all the time.

Cook's Tip If you have a potato masher, it gives a much more interesting texture to the purée; a liquidizer or food processor makes it too smooth.

Variation Many other root vegetables make excellent purées; try using swede, adding a little grated orange rind as well as the mixed spice.

VEGETABLE TIAN

preparation: 20 minutes

cooking: about 50 minutes

oven temperature: 190°C, 375°F, Gas Mark 5

serves 4

4 tablespoons olive oil

1 medium onion, peeled and thinly sliced

2 leeks, split, cleaned and cut into strips

1 red pepper, cored, seeded and sliced

1 yellow pepper, cored, seeded and sliced

1 medium aubergine, thinly sliced

2 garlic cloves, peeled and finely chopped

salt and freshly ground black pepper

6 medium courgettes, topped and tailed, and cut into slices

8 firm tomatoes, sliced

1 tablespoon chopped rosemary

3 tablespoons grated Parmesan cheese

1 Heat 2 tablespoons of the olive oil in a frying pan; add the onion and leeks and fry until lightly browned.

2 Add the peppers, aubergine and garlic, and fry gently until the vegetables are soft. Season to taste with salt and pepper.

3 Spoon the mixture into a greased ovenproof dish; arrange the courgettes and tomatoes attractively on the top.

4 Sprinkle with 1 tablespoon of the olive oil and the rosemary; bake in the preheated oven for 25 minutes.

5 Sprinkle the remaining olive oil and the Parmesan cheese over the top; bake in the oven for a further 10–15 minutes.

6 Serve piping hot.

Cook's Tip This is a very economical dish to prepare in greater quantities when entertaining large numbers of people. Serve it with a selection of cold meats or smoked fish, and a green salad.

Variation Try adding other vegetables such as sliced mushrooms, small French beans or spinach.

SPINACH WITH PINE KERNELS

preparation: 10 minutes

cooking: 5—6 minutes

serves 4

750 g/1½ lb fresh spinach, well washed

15 g/½ oz butter

1 garlic clove, peeled and finely chopped

2 tablespoons pine kernels

salt and freshly ground black pepper

freshly ground nutmeg

2 eggs, beaten

1 Shake all the excess moisture out of the spinach; put it into a pan with the butter, garlic, pine kernels, and salt, pepper and nutmeg to taste. Cover and cook for about 3—4 minutes, until the spinach loses its shape and starts to soften.

2 Tip the spinach into a sieve and press to extract the excess moisture.

3 Return the cooked spinach to a clean pan and stir in the beaten eggs; cook over a gentle heat, stirring, until the eggs scramble lightly and the spinach is hot.

4 Serve immediately, seasoning with extra salt, pepper and nutmeg if necessary.

Cook's Tip It is very important not to overcook the spinach, as it quickly loses its characteristic flavour and texture.

Variation Stir a little quark into the hot, cooked spinach instead of the beaten eggs.

GREEK-STYLE MIXED VEGETABLES

preparation: 10 minutes

cooking: 25 minutes

serves 4

1 medium onion, peeled and finely chopped

3 tablespoons olive oil

2 garlic cloves, peeled and finely chopped

1 tablespoon chopped marjoram

2 crushed bay leaves

strip of lemon peel

1 teaspoon coriander seeds

200 ml/⅓ pint dry white wine

½ small cauliflower, divided into florets

1 medium red pepper, cored, seeded and cut into 2.5 cm/1 inch chunks

1 medium green pepper, cored, seeded and cut into 2.5 cm/1 inch chunks

3 medium courgettes, topped, tailed and cut into 1 cm/½ inch chunks

100 g/4 oz button mushrooms

12 small green olives

1 Fry the onion in the olive oil with the garlic in a deep frying pan over a gentle heat for 3 minutes.

2 Add the marjoram, bay leaves, lemon peel, coriander seeds and white wine; bring to the boil and simmer for 2—3 minutes.

3 Add the cauliflower florets and simmer, covered, for 5 minutes.

4 Add the red and green peppers and courgettes, and simmer gently for a further 5 minutes.

5 Add the mushrooms and the green olives, and simmer for a further 5 minutes.

6 Season to taste with salt and pepper, and serve piping hot.

Cook's Tip This is an excellent way of using up leftover, uncooked vegetables, for example, half a cauliflower, or a few button mushrooms. There is no need to stick to the exact quantities given above, as long as the total weight of vegetables is about the same.

Variation This dish is equally good served chilled.

TOMATO AND FETA TARTS

preparation: 20 minutes

cooking: about 50 minutes

oven temperature: 190°C, 375°F, Gas Mark 5

serves 6

250 g/12 oz Lean Pastry (page 140)

750 g/1½ lb tomatoes, skinned, seeded and chopped

1 small onion, peeled and finely chopped

2 garlic cloves, peeled and chopped

1 tablespoon chopped basil

salt and freshly ground black pepper

2 tablespoons tomato paste

2 teaspoons chopped thyme

100 g/4 oz Feta cheese, crumbled

12 plump black olives

6 anchovy fillets, split lengthways

3 tablespoons olive oil

1 Roll out the pastry thinly; remember that Lean Pastry is not quite as easy to handle as standard shortcrust pastry. Using a fluted pastry cutter stamp out circles and use to line twelve individual patty tins; press up the edges well.
2 Put the tomatoes, onion, garlic, basil, salt and pepper to taste, tomato paste and thyme into a shallow pan; simmer for about 20 minutes until thick and pulpy.
3 Divide the tomato filling between the pastry cases, adding a little Feta to each one. Roll each black olive in a strip of anchovy fillet and place one on each tart. Dribble over a little olive oil.
4 Bake the tarts in the preheated oven for 25–30 minutes until the filling is a rich red colour, and the pastry has taken on some of the colour from the filling.
5 Serve immediately, allowing two per person.

Cook's Tip These little tarts make an unusual accompaniment to roast chicken or turkey, and add a dash of colour when arranged on the same platter. They freeze very well and are a good standby to have on hand.
Variation Crumbled Feta cheese is an acquired taste; for a milder flavour, top each tart with a sliver of Mozzarella cheese instead.

CABBAGE WITH SUNFLOWER SEEDS AND YOGURT

preparation: 10 minutes

cooking: 8 minutes

serves 4

1 small onion, peeled and thinly sliced

3 tablespoons olive oil

1 tablespoon sunflower seeds

2 garlic cloves, peeled and finely chopped

2 celery sticks, cut into matchstick strips

350 g/12 oz spring cabbage, finely shredded

3 tablespoons chicken stock (page 137)

2 tablespoons homemade yogurt (page 139)

salt and freshly ground black pepper

1 Fry the onion briskly in the oil for 1 minute; add the sunflower seeds, garlic and celery, and fry briskly for a further minute.
2 Add the shredded cabbage and stir-fry for a further 4 minutes.
3 Add the stock and bubble briskly for 1 minute.
4 Stir in the yogurt, and salt and pepper to taste, and heat through.
5 Serve piping hot.

Cook's Tip For the best results, use a wok; alternatively use a deep frying pan with curved sides.
Variation You can use Chinese leaves instead of spring cabbage; they will cook a little more quickly.

Tomato and Feta Tarts: *Tiny pastry shells hold a rich-red cheese and tomato filling.*

STIR-FRIED CHINESE LEAVES

preparation: 10 minutes

cooking: 6 minutes

serves 4

3 tablespoons olive oil

1 medium onion, peeled and finely chopped

2 garlic cloves, peeled and cut into thin strips

½ medium head Chinese leaves, finely shredded

1 teaspoon coriander seeds

2 tablespoons salted cashew nuts

2 tablespoons chopped coriander

freshly ground black pepper

1 Heat the olive oil in a deep frying pan or wok; add the onion and garlic, and stir-fry for 2 minutes over a high heat.
2 Add the Chinese leaves, coriander seeds, cashew nuts, half the coriander, and pepper to taste; stir-fry for a further 4 minutes.
3 Serve piping hot, sprinkled with the remaining coriander.

Cook's Tip It is important to keep the ingredients moving when stir-frying so that they cook quickly and evenly, but still retain their texture.
Variation Use equal quantities of Chinese leaves and shredded fresh spinach, but only cook the spinach for the final minute.

POTATO AND HAZELNUT BAKE

preparation: 20 minutes

cooking: 35−40 minutes

oven temperature: 190°C, 375°F, Gas Mark 5

serves 4

550 g/1¼ lb potatoes, peeled

1 small onion, peeled and finely chopped

2 tablespoons chopped parsley

3 tablespoons chopped hazelnuts

salt and freshly ground black pepper

150 ml/¼ pint chicken stock (page 137)

150 ml/¼ pint skimmed milk

2 eggs

1 Slice the potatoes very thinly; use a mandolin or the slicing blade on a food processor for speed.
2 Layer the potato slices with the onion, parsley, 2 tablespoons of the chopped hazelnuts, and salt and pepper to taste in a greased deep ovenproof dish.
3 Beat the stock with the skimmed milk, eggs, and salt and pepper to taste; pour over the potatoes and sprinkle with the remaining hazelnuts.
4 Cover with foil and bake in the preheated oven for 25 minutes; remove the foil and bake for a further 10−15 minutes, until the potatoes are pale golden and tender.

Cook's Tip If you have to slice the potatoes by hand with a sharp knife, they will be slightly thicker, and consequently will take longer to cook.
Variation Add a little grated cheese as well as the chopped nuts between each layer of potatoes; choose a variety that does not have too strong a flavour.

LEEK SOUFFLE

preparation: 20 minutes

cooking: about 40 minutes

oven temperature: 190°C, 375°F, Gas Mark 5

serves 4

2 medium leeks, split, cleaned and cut into

thin strips

40 g/1½ oz butter

1 garlic clove, peeled and crushed

40 g/1½ oz plain flour

300 ml/½ pint skimmed milk

salt and freshly ground black pepper

3 egg yolks

4 egg whites

2 tablespoons grated Parmesan cheese

1 Cook the leeks gently in the butter with the garlic for about 3 minutes; stir in the flour and cook for 1 minute.

2 Gradually stir in the milk and bring to the boil, stirring, and simmer until the sauce has thickened. Season to taste with salt and pepper.

3 Remove the sauce from the heat and beat in the egg yolks. Whisk the egg whites until stiff but not dry, and fold lightly but thoroughly into the sauce mixture, together with 1 tablespoon of the grated Parmesan.

4 Carefully transfer the mixture to a well-greased 18 cm/7 inch soufflé dish.

5 Sprinkle with the remaining Parmesan cheese. Bake in the pre-heated oven for about 35 minutes, until well risen, just set and golden.

6 Serve immediately with hot Tomato Sauce (page 138) as an accompaniment.

Cook's Tip One of the secrets with any hot soufflé is not to overbeat the egg whites; they should hold their shape, but not be so stiff that they will not blend evenly with the other ingredients.

Variation Courgettes also make a delicious soufflé. Top, tail and shred 4 medium courgettes, fry gently in the butter and proceed as above.

OKRA IN SPICY TOMATO SAUCE

preparation: 10 minutes

cooking: 20 minutes

serves 4

300 ml/½ pint Tomato Sauce

(page 138)

2 fresh green chillies, sliced

1 tablespoon chopped fresh coriander

small piece of cinnamon stick, crushed

salt and freshly ground black pepper

150 ml/¼ pint homemade yogurt

(page 139)

350 g/12 oz small okra, trimmed

1 Put the Tomato Sauce, chillies, coriander, cinnamon stick, and salt and pepper to taste into a deep frying pan; bring to the boil and simmer gently for 5 minutes.

2 Add the yogurt and the okra; cover the pan and simmer very gently for 15 minutes, until the okra is tender but not too soft.

3 Serve piping hot, with a bowl of chilled yogurt as an accompaniment, if liked.

Cook's Tip Okra contain a very gummy liquid; when trimming them, it is important to take only a small piece off the stalk end, without cutting into the stem part as this would release the liquid, making the sauce very glutinous.

Variation Instead of adding yogurt to the sauce, whisk in some small knobs of low-fat cheese.

PUREED FRESH PEAS WITH GINGER

preparation: 6 minutes

cooking: 15−20 minutes

serves 4

450 g/1 lb shelled peas, fresh or frozen

piece of fresh root ginger, bruised

150 ml/¼ pint chicken stock (page 137)

pinch of ground mace

salt and freshly ground black pepper

2 egg yolks

1 tablespoon homemade yogurt (page 139)

1 Put the peas into a shallow pan with the ginger, stock, mace, and salt and pepper to taste; cover and simmer gently until the peas are tender and the stock has almost evaporated.
2 Put the pea mixture into a liquidizer or food processor with the egg yolks and yogurt; blend until smooth and then adjust seasoning to taste.
3 Heat the purée through gently in a saucepan.

Cook's Tip The amount of liquid used in this recipe is quite small, so watch carefully to ensure that it does not evaporate completely during cooking. If necessary add a little extra stock.
Variation This purée is delicious made with shelled young broad beans when they are in season.

ASPARAGUS WITH ORANGE SAUCE

preparation: 20 minutes

cooking: 15−20 minutes

serves 4

750 g/1½ lb young asparagus

2 egg yolks

finely grated rind and juice of ½ orange

6 tablespoons olive oil

2 tablespoons chopped parsley

3 tablespoons crème fraîche

salt and freshly ground black pepper

to garnish:

peeled orange segments

1 Trim the asparagus spears if necessary so that they are all the same length; tie together in a neat bundle.
2 Beat the egg yolks with the orange rind and juice; gradually whisk in the olive oil as if making mayonnaise. Stir in the parsley, crème fraîche, and salt and pepper to taste.
3 Stand the bundle of asparagus upright in an asparagus steamer or in a deep saucepan, and add sufficient boiling water to come 7.5 cm/3 inch up the asparagus stems. Cook, covered, for 15−20 minutes, until the asparagus stems are just tender.
4 Meanwhile heat the prepared sauce through in a basin over a pan of hot water.
5 Drain the cooked asparagus thoroughly and place on a warm serving dish; spoon the sauce across the asparagus.
6 Garnish with orange segments and serve immediately.

Cook's Tip If you do not have an asparagus steamer, a double saucepan makes a very good substitute. Stand the bundle of asparagus in the base pan and add the correct amount of boiling water; invert the inner saucepan over the top of the asparagus so that it balances evenly on the base pan. Cook for the time given above.
Variation To serve the asparagus cold, cook as above, drain well and marinate in a little olive oil mixed with fresh orange juice, and salt and pepper to taste. Serve with the same orange sauce.

Asparagus with Orange Sauce: *No melted butter, no Hollandaise;
tender asparagus is served here with a fresh orange sauce.*

CARROT AND COURGETTE CUTLETS

preparation: 30 minutes, plus chilling

cooking: 10–12 minutes

serves 4

350 g/12 oz carrots, peeled

350 g/12 oz courgettes, topped and tailed

finely grated rind of ½ lemon

2 tablespoons chopped parsley

1 tablespoon chopped chives

2 tablespoons chopped nuts, toasted

6 tablespoons fresh wholemeal breadcrumbs

1 whole egg

1 egg yolk

salt and freshly ground black pepper

flour for dusting

beaten egg

75 g/3 oz almonds, chopped

2 tablespoons melted butter

1 Put the carrots and courgettes through the shredder blade of a food processor; alternatively grate them coarsely.

2 Mix the vegetables with the lemon rind, parsley, chives, nuts, breadcrumbs, whole egg and egg yolk, work together to a smooth mixture. Season to taste with salt and pepper.

3 Shape into eight small cutlets, using floured hands; dip into beaten egg and then coat evenly with almonds. Chill for 1 hour.

4 Brush the carrot and courgette cutlets on one side with melted butter; cook under a preheated grill for about 5 minutes; turn the cutlets over, brush once again with melted butter and grill for a further 5 minutes.

5 Serve hot with Herb and Lemon Sauce (page 138).

Cook's Tip Vegetables vary in their moisture content; if the above mixture seems a little too dry when you mould it, add an extra egg yolk.

Variation Add 50 g/2 oz grated mature Cheddar to the basic mixture, prior to moulding.

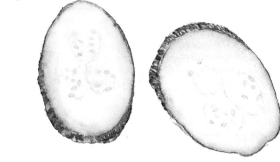

SWEET-SOUR ONIONS

preparation: 10 minutes

cooking: about 25 minutes

serves 4

300 ml/½ pint Tomato Sauce (page 138)

1 teaspoon pink or green peppercorns

1 small onion, peeled and very finely chopped

1 teaspoon chopped fresh thyme

2 tablespoons red wine

finely grated rind of ½ orange

1 teaspoon Worcestershire sauce

salt

350 g/12 oz small button onions, peeled

to garnish:

bay leaves

1 Put the Tomato Sauce into a shallow pan with the peppercorns, onion, thyme, red wine, orange rind and Worcestershire sauce; bring to the boil and season to taste with salt.

2 Add the button onions; cover and simmer gently until they are glazed and just tender.

3 Serve either hot or chilled, garnished with bay leaves.

Cook's Tip Peel the onions under cold running water to prevent them from bringing tears to your eyes.

Variation Prepare the same sauce and add small firm button mushrooms instead of the onions, cooking for only 6–8 minutes.

Carrot and Courgette Cutlets: *Little cakes of shredded vegetables with a crisp nut coating.* **Sweet–Sour Onions:** *Tiny button onions deliciously glazed with a tangy tomato sauce.*

55

STUFFED MUSHROOMS

preparation: 15 minutes

cooking: 25 minutes

oven temperature: 190°C, 375°F, Gas Mark 5

serves 4

1 small onion, peeled and finely chopped

2 tablespoons olive oil

1 garlic clove, peeled and crushed

12 medium flat mushrooms

salt and freshly ground black pepper

4 tablespoons fresh wholemeal
breadcrumbs

2 tablespoons finely chopped walnuts

1 tablespoon chopped parsley

2 teaspoons chopped marjoram

1 egg, beaten

2 tablespoons Sage Derby cheese, grated

1 Fry the onion gently in the oil with the garlic for 3 minutes.
2 Remove the stalks from the mushrooms and chop them; peel the mushrooms.
3 Add the mushroom stalks to the onion and fry together for about 2 minutes.
4 Season to taste and mix in the breadcrumbs, walnuts, parsley, marjoram, beaten egg and cheese.
5 Place the mushrooms, stalk side uppermost, in a lightly greased ovenproof dish; top each mushroom with some of the stuffing, mounding it neatly.
6 Bake the mushrooms in the preheated oven for about 20 minutes.
7 Serve hot.

Cook's Tip If the mushrooms are in really good condition and do not have dirty skins, there is no need to peel them.
Variation Add a little finely chopped lean ham to the stuffing to make the dish rather more substantial.

SOUFFLEED AUBERGINES

preparation: 30 minutes, plus standing

cooking: about 40 minutes

oven temperature: 190°C, 375°F, Gas Mark 5

serves 4

2 medium aubergines, cut in half
lengthways

salt and freshly ground black pepper

1 small onion, peeled and finely chopped

2 tablespoons olive oil

1 garlic clove, peeled and crushed

3 tablespoons fresh wholemeal
breadcrumbs

50 g/2 oz curd cheese

2 eggs, separated

3 tablespoons grated Parmesan cheese

1 Score the flesh of the aubergines criss-cross and sprinkle with salt. Turn cut surfaces down on paper towels and leave to drain for 30 minutes.
2 Rinse, then carefully scoop out the aubergine flesh, leaving shells about 5 mm/¼ inch thick; chop the aubergine flesh quite finely.
3 Fry the onion gently in the oil for 3 minutes; add the garlic and aubergine flesh and fry for a further 3−4 minutes.
4 Mix in the wholemeal breadcrumbs, curd cheese, salt and pepper to taste, egg yolks and 1 tablespoon of the Parmesan cheese.
5 Whisk the egg whites until stiff but not dry, and fold lightly but thoroughly into the aubergine mixture.
6 Place the aubergine shells in a lightly greased ovenproof dish and fill with the souffléed aubergine mixture; sprinkle with the remaining Parmesan cheese.
7 Bake in the preheated oven for 30−35 minutes, until puffed, risen and golden. Serve immediately, either on their own, or with Tomato Sauce (page 138).

Cook's Tip The easiest way of hollowing out the aubergines is to use a grapefruit knife with a serrated edge.
Variation Instead of using curd cheese and breadcrumbs, a little flaked cooked fish or chopped chicken can be added to the soufflé mixture.

CHICORY IN LIGHT CHEESE SAUCE

preparation: about 15 minutes

cooking: about 30 minutes

oven temperature: 190°C, 375°F, Gas Mark 5

serves 4

●

8 small chicory heads

salt and freshly ground black pepper

1 small onion, peeled and finely chopped

1 garlic clove, peeled and crushed

1 tablespoon olive oil

200 ml/⅓ pint dry white wine

2 bay leaves, crushed

4 tablespoons fromage blanc (page 140)

2 egg yolks

50 g/2 oz curd cheese

freshly ground nutmeg

to garnish:

paprika

1 Put the chicory heads into a large pan of boiling salted water and blanch for 1 minute; drain and immediately plunge into a bowl of cold water.

2 Fry the chopped onion and garlic gently in the olive oil for 3 minutes; place in the bottom of a lightly greased ovenproof dish and lay the drained heads of chicory on top.

3 Add the white wine, bay leaves, and salt and pepper to taste. Cover with foil and cook in the preheated oven for about 20 minutes until just tender, but still with a good texture.

4 Remove the cooked chicory to a serving dish and keep warm.

5 Strain the cooking liquid into the top of a double saucepan; add the fromage blanc, egg yolks and curd cheese. Whisk over simmering water until the sauce is lightly thickened and smooth. Season with nutmeg, salt and pepper.

6 Spoon the sauce evenly over the chicory and sprinkle with a little paprika. Serve hot.

Cook's Tip Some people find chicory rather bitter; if liked, you can add a teaspoon of brown sugar with the wine.

Variation Hearts of cos lettuce are delicious topped with this sauce; cook them in the wine liquid for only about 6 minutes.

FONDUE PEPPERS

preparation: 15 minutes

cooking: 35 minutes

oven temperature: 190°C, 375°F, Gas Mark 5

serves 4

●

4 medium red peppers

1 large onion, peeled and finely chopped

2 garlic cloves, peeled and finely chopped

2 tablespoons olive oil

2 tablespoons chopped basil

1 tablespoon chopped parsley

salt and freshly ground black pepper

175 g/6 oz Mozzarella cheese, cut into thin slivers

to garnish:

sprigs of fresh basil

1 Cut the peppers in half crossways; trim off the stalks, and remove the centre seeds and membrane.

2 Stand the pepper halves upright in a lightly greased ovenproof dish.

3 Fry the onion and garlic gently in the oil for about 4 minutes; mix in the basil, parsley, and salt and pepper to taste.

4 Divide the onion and herb mixture between the pepper halves; add some slivers of Mozzarella to the centre of each one.

5 Cover with foil and bake in the preheated oven for about 30 minutes.

6 Serve piping hot, garnished with sprigs of fresh basil.

Cook's Tip Make sure that you do not make a hole in the peppers when you remove the stalks, as the cheese would then seep out during cooking.

Variation You need rather sweet peppers for this recipe; the green ones are not really suitable, but yellow ones make a good alternative.

WARM VEGETABLE PLATTER

preparation: 30 minutes

cooking: 15 minutes

serves 4

300 ml/½ pint chicken stock (page 137)

16 small new potatoes, scrubbed

12 small new carrots, scrubbed

8 baby courgettes

2 small fennel heads, halved or quartered

175 g/6 oz mangetout

sprig of tarragon

sprig of thyme

juice of ½ lemon

mousseline:

2 egg yolks

juice of ½ lemon

150 ml/¼ pint olive oil

½ teaspoon French mustard

2 large garlic cloves, peeled and finely crushed

salt and freshly ground black pepper

to garnish (optional):

4 small gherkins, fanned

1 tablespoon capers

wedges of lemon

1 To make the mousseline, put the egg yolks into a bowl and beat with the lemon juice; gradually whisk in the olive oil, little by little, as if making mayonnaise. Add the mustard, garlic, and salt and pepper to taste. Cover and keep cool.

2 Put the chicken stock into a large pan and bring to the boil; add the potatoes in a single layer and then the carrots.

3 Cover the pan and cook for 5 minutes. Add the courgettes and fennel and cook, covered, for a further 5 minutes.

4 Add the mangetout, tarragon and thyme and cook, covered, for 3 minutes.

5 Drain the cooked vegetables and arrange in sections on a warmed platter; season to taste with salt and pepper and sprinkle with lemon juice.

6 Serve the hot vegetables garnished with gherkins, capers and lemon wedges if liked, and accompanied by the garlic mousseline.

Cook's Tip The mousseline can be made in a liquidizer if preferred; it is still necessary to add the olive oil gradually.

Variation To turn this warm vegetable platter into a main meal, simply add 100 g/4 oz poached white fish or chicken per person.

COURGETTES IN WALNUT SAUCE

preparation: 20 minutes

cooking: 7−8 minutes

serves 4

450 g/1 lb courgettes, topped and tailed

100 g/4 oz walnut pieces

300 ml/½ pint chicken stock (page 137)

2 tablespoons roughly chopped parsley

2 garlic cloves, peeled

salt and freshly ground black pepper

grated rind of ½ lemon

1 Slice the courgettes very thinly; use a mandolin, or the slicer blade of a food processor if you have one.

2 Put the courgettes into a steamer and steam for 5 minutes.

3 Meanwhile prepare the sauce: put the walnuts, chicken stock, parsley, garlic, salt and pepper to taste, and the lemon rind into a liquidizer or food processor; blend until smooth.

4 Pour the prepared sauce into a large shallow pan; add the drained steamed courgettes and heat through gently.

Cook's Tip If you do not have a steamer, stand a metal colander over a pan of gently simmering water and cover with a lid or foil.

Variation This recipe is also very good made with carrots; they will take a few minutes longer to cook.

Warm Vegetable Platter with Garlic Mousseline: *A platter of warm, lightly cooked vegetables flavoured with herbs and served with a garlic sauce*

Fish & Shellfish

Fish and shellfish are among the healthiest foods that we eat. They are an excellent source of protein; they are much lower in saturated fats than red meat; and it is now thought that fish oil may play a valuable part in improving coronary health. Furthermore, calcium is derived from the edible bones of tiny fish like whitebait. So it is not surprising that fish have moved to the top of the main course league in many health-conscious families.

The five basic categories of fish are white fish, oily fish, freshwater fish, smoked fish and shellfish. White fish are classified either as flat, like plaice, or round, like cod. Oily fish include mackerel and herrings. Some freshwater fish spend all their time in rivers and lakes, whereas others are spawned in the sea but move to a river to grow. Carp, bream and trout are true freshwater fish, but the salmon, for example, is one of the hybrids. Smoked fish range from the delicious but expensive smoked Scottish salmon to the economical kipper. Shellfish or *fruits de mer* extend from mussels to lobsters, the royalty of crustaceans.

Only buy fish that are very fresh and preferably cook or use on the same day. This applies particularly to shellfish. Always cover fish tightly with cling film before storing in the refrigerator to prevent the smell spreading to other foods.

Most fish require very careful, brief cooking otherwise the texture, flavour and shape can be completely spoiled. Poaching is one of the cooking methods best suited to fish, as it is fast yet gentle.

The fish recipes in *Lean Cuisine* include marinated fish, which requires no cooking, and whole trout cooked in a paper bag. But the chapter's highlight is perhaps the Antibes Saffron Stew — a memorable dish, inspired by the delicious Provençal versions that I have enjoyed along the Mediterranean coast.

SALMON IN VINE LEAVES

preparation: 30 minutes

cooking: 45—50 minutes

oven temperature: 190°C, 375°F, Gas Mark 5

serves 6—8

1 × 1.75 kg/4 lb salmon or sea trout, head
and tail removed,

filleted but not skinned

salt and freshly ground black pepper

75 g/3 oz curd cheese

1 garlic clove, peeled and crushed

finely grated rind of 1 lemon

2 tablespoons chopped dill

10 vine leaves, soaked in warm water for
15—20 minutes

300 ml/½ pint dry white wine

1 lemon, thinly sliced

sauce:

150 ml/¼ pint homemade yogurt (page 139)

1 tablespoon orange lumpfish roe

1 tablespoon chopped dill

to garnish:

thin slices of orange or lemon

1 Lay the fillets flesh-side uppermost, and season with salt and pepper.
2 Mix the curd cheese with the garlic, lemon rind and dill; spread over one fillet and lay the second fillet on top.
3 Wrap the sandwiched fish in vine leaves, so as to completely enclose it. The easiest way to do this is to lay half the vine leaves in a large shallow ovenproof dish and then put the prepared fish on the top; lay the remaining vine leaves over the fish and tuck the ends neatly underneath.
4 Pour over the white wine, top with the orange or lemon slices, and cover with foil. Bake in the preheated oven for 45—50 minutes.
5 Remove from the oven and leave the fish to stand, covered, for 10 minutes.
6 Meanwhile make the sauce: mix the yogurt with the lumpfish roe and the dill; season to taste with salt and pepper.
7 Lift the fish carefully out of the baking dish and place on a large oval platter. Garnish with fresh slices of orange or lemon.
8 To serve, fold back the top vine leaves and cut through the stuffed fish in sections. Serve accompanied by the sauce.

Cook's Tip Vine leaves vary in quality; some are much tougher than others, and some are much stronger in flavour. If they are packed in brine, rinse them very well to remove the excess salt. Tear the corner off one leaf; if it seems unduly tough, blanch the vine leaves in simmering water for 6—8 minutes before using, to soften them slightly.
Variation To serve cold at a buffet party, allow the fish to cool completely in its vine leaf wrapping, and then lift it onto a serving dish. Cut into sections with the fish still wrapped in vine leaves; the colour contrast looks very pretty.

TROUT IN A PAPER BAG

preparation: 30 minutes

cooking: 35—40 minutes

oven temperature: 190°C, 375°F, Gas Mark 5

serves 4

4 medium trout (about 200 g/7 oz each),
cleaned

salt and freshly ground black pepper

4 tablespoons olive oil

2 garlic cloves, peeled and finely chopped

1 tablespoon chopped thyme

1 tablespoon chopped rosemary

150 ml/¼ pint rosé wine

1 Cut eight rectangles of greaseproof paper, double the width of each trout, and half as long again as the fish. Brush one side of each rectangle with oil.
2 Place four rectangles on a baking sheet, oiled side uppermost. Lay a trout along the centre of each one; pull up the edges of the paper and staple at each corner so that the paper forms a container for each fish.
3 Sprinkle a little olive oil, salt and pepper, garlic and herbs over each trout; spoon 2 tablespoons of the rosé wine over each one.
4 Cover with the remaining pieces of greaseproof paper, oiled side down; staple at the corners as before to form a lid over each fish. Staple the top and bottom layers of greaseproof paper together in two or three places.
5 Bake in the preheated oven for 35—40 minutes, until the fish is cooked and the paper has started to brown.
6 Take the fish to the table in the paper parcels; open the parcels at the table to release the delicious aroma.

Cook's Tip It is essential that the paper parcels enclose the trout loosely; the paper contracts in the heat and if the fish were tightly wrapped, the 'bags' would split.
Variation Red mullet or very small sea bass can also be used.

Salmon Trout in Vine Leaves: *A whole filleted salmon is sandwiched*
with a curd cheese, garlic and dill stuffing and cooked in a parcel of vine leaves.

MARINATED TROUT WITH OLIVES

preparation: 10 minutes, plus chilling
cooking: about 10 minutes
serves 4

4 tablespoons olive oil

4 small trout, filleted

salt and freshly ground black pepper

1 small onion, peeled and finely chopped

2 garlic cloves, peeled and finely chopped

150 ml/¼ pint dry white wine

1 medium yellow pepper, cored, seeded
and cut into thin strips

1 tablespoon chopped basil

12 green olives (preferably the type stuffed
with almonds)

1 Heat 2 tablespoons of the olive oil in a large non-stick pan; add the trout fillets and fry for 1−2 minutes on each side, turning the fillets over very carefully.
2 Place the trout fillets in a shallow serving dish and season with salt and pepper.
3 Fry the onion and garlic gently in the remaining olive oil for 3−4 minutes; add the white wine, strips of yellow pepper and the basil, and simmer gently for 3 minutes.
4 Stir in the green olives and spoon the marinade evenly over the fish. Cover and chill for 3−4 hours.

Cook's Tip Ask your fishmonger to do the filleting for you; he will do it more quickly and easily.
Variation Other small fish such as red mullet, sole and plaice can be filleted and prepared in exactly the same way.

MEDITERRANEAN-STYLE MACKEREL

preparation: 10 minutes
cooking: 50−55 minutes
oven temperature: 180°C, 350°F, Gas Mark 4
serves 4

1 medium onion, peeled and thinly sliced

3 tablespoons olive oil

450 g/1 lb tomatoes, skinned, seeded and
chopped

200 ml/⅓ pint red wine

2 garlic cloves, peeled and chopped

1 tablespoon chopped basil

salt and freshly ground black pepper

1 medium red pepper, cored and seeded

1 medium aubergine, cut into small cubes

50 g/2 oz stoned black olives, sliced

4 medium mackerel (about 250 g/9 oz
each), cleaned and gutted

to garnish:

chopped basil or parsley

1 Fry the onion gently in the oil for 3−4 minutes; add the tomatoes, red wine, garlic, basil, salt and pepper to taste, and simmer for 5 minutes.
2 Add the finely chopped red pepper, aubergine, and black olives and simmer for a further 6 minutes.
3 Lay the mackerel in a fairly deep ovenproof dish and spoon the prepared sauce evenly over the top.
4 Cover the dish and bake in the preheated oven for about 40−45 minutes, until the fish are tender.
5 Remove the fish and sauce to a rimmed serving dish and serve piping hot, sprinkled with basil or parsley.

Cook's Tip It is traditional to leave the heads on mackerel, but you may remove them before cooking, if preferred.
Variation Plump rainbow trout or red mullet can be cooked in exactly the same way.

MEXICAN-STYLE FISH

preparation: 15 minutes, plus chilling

serves 4

450 g/1 lb sole fillets, skinned

1 small onion, peeled and thinly sliced

1 tablespoon crushed coriander seeds

juice of 4 limes

finely grated rind of 2 limes

3 tablespoons olive oil

3 tablespoons dry white wine

salt and freshly ground black pepper

2 garlic cloves, peeled and finely chopped

to garnish:

1 green pepper, cored, seeded and cut into thin strips

12 cooked, unpeeled prawns

1 Cut the sole fillets into long thin strips; put them into a shallow dish with the onion rings and coriander seeds.
2 Mix the lime juice with the lime rind, olive oil, white wine, salt and pepper to taste, and the garlic; spoon evenly over the sole strips.
3 Cover the fish and chill for at least 6 hours, until the fish turns opaque and looks 'cooked'. Turn the fish strips once or twice during this time.
4 Lift the marinated fish strips onto a serving dish and spoon over a little of the liquid. Garnish with the green pepper and the prawns.

Cook's Tip This makes a wonderfully light dish for a summer lunch: marinate the fish overnight and serve it well chilled, with a crisp sparkling dry white wine.
Variation Stir in a few slices of peeled avocado after the fish has marinated. Allow 1 avocado per four servings.

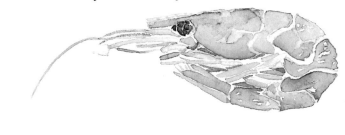

CHILLED FISH CURRY

preparation: 20 minutes, plus chilling

cooking: about 13 minutes

serves 4

350 g/12 oz thick cod fillet

350 g/12 oz filleted salmon

150 ml/¼ pint fish stock (page 137)

150 ml/¼ pint dry white wine

3 spring onions, topped and tailed

1 tablespoon olive oil

1 tablespoon curry powder (page 141)

1 tablespoon mango chutney

200 ml/⅓ pint homemade yogurt (page 139)

salt and freshly ground black pepper

1 medium ripe mango, peeled, stoned and chopped (page 90)

to garnish:

paprika

wedges of lime

sprigs of fresh mint

1 Put the cod and salmon fillet into a deep frying pan; add the fish stock and white wine. Cover and poach gently for 10 minutes.
2 Lift the fish out carefully with a slotted spoon. Skin and flake it coarsely while it is still warm; reserve the cooking liquid.
3 Fry the finely chopped spring onions gently in the oil for 1 minute. Add the curry powder and cook for a further minute. Stir in 200 ml/⅓ pint of the fish cooking liquid and bring to the boil. Allow to cool.
4 Mix the cooled curry sauce with the chutney, yogurt, and salt and pepper to taste; stir in the fish carefully, together with the mango.
5 Cover the prepared fish curry and chill for at least 4 hours.
6 Spoon onto a shallow serving dish and garnish with a sprinkling of paprika, wedges of lime and sprigs of fresh mint.
7 Serve with cooked brown rice, mixed with a light oil and vinegar dressing, and chilled.

Cook's Tip It is very important not to overcook the fish; if the filleted fish is quite thin, reduce the cooking time accordingly.
Variation Try adding some shellfish, such as cooked shelled mussels, flaked cooked crabmeat, or, for a very special occasion, some thick flakes of cooked lobster.

BAKED RED MULLET WITH LIMES

preparation: 15 minutes

cooking: 25 minutes

oven temperature: 190°C, 375°F, Gas Mark 5

serves 4

4 medium red mullet (about 175 g/6 oz each), gutted and cleaned

finely grated rind and juice of 2 limes

1 teaspoon green peppercorns

salt

4 sprigs thyme

2 garlic cloves, peeled and finely chopped

2 tablespoons olive oil

to garnish:

thin wedges of lime

1 Make two to three cuts in the thickest part of each mullet.

2 Mix the lime rind with the green peppercorns and salt to taste; press a little of this mixture inside each mullet, together with a sprig of thyme.

3 Lay the mullet in a lightly greased ovenproof dish; sprinkle with the lime juice, garlic and olive oil, and cover with a piece of foil.

4 Bake in the preheated oven for 15 minutes; remove the foil and continue baking for a further 10 minutes.

5 Serve the mullet garnished with wedges of lime.

Cook's Tip Limes will grate more easily if they are cold, and if you use a coarse side of the grater.

Variation Small trout can be used if preferred.

POACHED FISH WITH GARLIC SAUCE

preparation: about 20 minutes

cooking: 10 minutes

serves 4

450 g/1 lb haddock fillet, skinned and cut into four portions

fish stock (page 137)

small bunch of parsley stalks

rind and juice of ½ lemon

salt and freshly ground black pepper

½ cauliflower, divided into florets

8 radishes

3 celery sticks, cut into 5 cm/2 inch lengths

12 tiny new potatoes, cooked in their skins

garlic sauce:

6 garlic cloves, peeled and crushed

2 egg yolks

6 tablespoons olive oil

150 ml/¼ pint homemade yogurt (page 139)

1 Put the haddock fillet into a deep frying pan; add fish stock to half cover the fish, the parsley stalks, thinly pared lemon rind, and salt and pepper to taste.

2 Cover and poach gently for 10 minutes. Leave the fish to stand in its cooking liquid, covered, while you prepare the sauce.

3 Beat the garlic with the egg yolks; beat in the olive oil in a fine trickle, until fully absorbed. Mix in the lemon juice and yogurt.

4 Drain the fish and place on a serving platter; arrange the florets of cauliflower, radishes, lengths of celery and potatoes around the warm fish.

5 Serve immediately with the garlic sauce.

Cook's Tip If you prefer, start off with 3–4 garlic cloves in the sauce and then add more if liked.

Variation This dish is equally good prepared with smoked haddock.

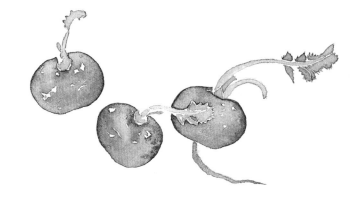

Baked Red Mullet with Limes: *Red Mullet, the prettiest of Mediterranean fish, are studded with lime, green peppercorns and fresh thyme before baking.*

67

COD CUTLETS WITH PERNOD SAUCE

preparation: 20 minutes

cooking: about 40 minutes

oven temperature: 190°C, 375°F, Gas Mark 5

serves 4

4 medium courgettes, topped, tailed and shredded

1 garlic clove, peeled and crushed

25 g/1 oz butter

salt and freshly ground black pepper

1 tablespoon chopped chives

4 medium cod cutlets, about 175 g/6 oz each

4 tablespoons Pernod

300 ml/½ pint Herb and Lemon Sauce (page 138)

1 tablespoon black lumpfish roe

1 Cook the courgettes and garlic gently in the butter for 3 minutes; add salt and pepper to taste and the chives.

2 Cut out eight squares of foil, each one slightly larger than the cod cutlets. When putting a cutlet in the centre, there should be a 4 cm/1½ inch border the whole way round.

3 Divide the cooked courgettes between four of the foil squares; put a cod cutlet in the centre of each one and pull up the edges of the foil slightly.

4 Sprinkle each cod cutlet with about 1½ teaspoons of the Pernod. Lay the remaining foil squares over the fish and pinch the edges of the foil securely together to seal.

5 Put the foil parcels on a baking sheet. Cook in the preheated oven for 30 minutes.

6 Put the remaining Pernod and the Herb and Lemon Sauce into the top of a double saucepan and heat through gently.

7 Put the foil parcels on a flat serving dish, and carefully remove the foil lid from each one; place a little black lumpfish roe on the top of each portion.

8 Serve immediately accompanied by the warm sauce.

Cook's Tip Wrap the cod cutlets loosely in the foil so that the fish cooks in its own steam.

Variation Pernod is very much an acquired taste; a dry vermouth can be used instead.

SKATE WITH CHIVES AND GRAPES

preparation: 10–15 minutes

cooking: about 13 minutes

serves 4

4 wing pieces of skate (about 1kg/2 lb in total)

1 tablespoon chopped chives

2 garlic cloves, peeled and finely chopped

200 ml/⅓ pint dry white wine

grated rind and juice of ½ lemon

1 teaspoon white peppercorns

salt

3 tablespoons homemade yogurt (page 139)

100 g/4 oz seedless green grapes, skinned, if wished

to garnish

chopped chives

1 Put the pieces of skate into a large shallow pan with the chives, garlic, white wine, lemon rind and juice, peppercorns, and salt to taste.

2 Cover the pan and bring to the boil; simmer gently for 10 minutes, until the fish are cooked.

3 Lift the pieces of skate carefully onto a warm serving dish, and keep warm.

4 Boil the cooking liquid briskly until reduced by half. Stir in the yogurt and the grapes, and heat through gently without re-boiling.

5 Spoon the sauce over the skate, garnish with chopped chives, and serve immediately.

Cook's Tip Skate is one of the most gelatinous types of fish; soak the pan as soon as you have finished cooking the skate and you will find it much easier to clean.

Variation Skate tastes very good with capers; omit the grapes and add 1 tablespoon of capers to the sauce instead.

FISH AND AUBERGINE PIE

preparation: about 20 minutes

cooking: about 1 hour

oven temperature: 190°C, 375°F, Gas Mark 5

serves 4

2 medium aubergines, thinly sliced

2 tablespoons olive oil

450 g/1 lb haddock or cod fillet

300 ml/½ pint fish stock (page 137)

25 g/1 oz butter

2 leeks, split, cleaned and chopped

100 g/4 oz button mushrooms, chopped

1½ tablespoons wholemeal flour

150 ml/¼ pint skimmed milk

2 tablespoons chopped parsley

150 ml/¼ pint yogurt (page 139)

1 egg

50 g/2 oz grated Edam or Gouda cheese

1 Lay the aubergines on a lightly greased baking sheet in a single layer; brush with the olive oil. Bake in the preheated oven for 8 minutes.

2 Put the fish fillet into a deep frying pan with the fish stock and salt and pepper to taste; cover and poach gently for about 8 minutes until the fish is tender. Carefully drain the fish from its cooking liquid and flake coarsely; reserve the cooking liquid.

3 Melt the butter in a pan; add the leeks and mushrooms and fry gently for 3 minutes. Stir in the flour and cook for 1 minute.

4 Gradually stir in 150 ml/¼ pint of the fish cooking liquid and the skimmed milk. Bring to the boil, stirring, and simmer until the sauce has thickened. Add the parsley and lightly mix in the cooked fish.

5 Transfer the fish mixture to a lightly-greased, deep gratin dish; arrange the aubergine on top.

6 Beat the yogurt with the egg and spoon evenly over the aubergine; sprinkle with the cheese.

7 Bake in the preheated oven for 30−35 minutes until golden brown. Serve piping hot.

Cook's Tip Take care not to overcook the fish initially as this will ruin the final texture; if the fish fillets are very thin, reduce the cooking time slightly.

Variation The dish is very good made with smoked haddock or cod fillet.

SCALLOPINES OF SALMON WITH RASPBERRY VINEGAR

preparation: 20 minutes, plus chilling

serves 4

350 g/12 oz boned salmon, in one piece

1 large avocado, halved, stoned, peeled, and thinly sliced

juice 1 lemon

4 tablespoons raspberry vinegar

2 tablespoons olive oil

1 clove garlic, finely crushed

salt and freshly ground black pepper

1 teaspoon pink peppercorns

4 pastry tartlets (page 48)

shredded courgette, tossed in Yogurt Mayonnaise (page 139)

red lumpfish roe

1 Using a very sharp knife, cut the salmon into thin slivers; lay them out in a single layer between two sheets of cling film until needed. (This can be done up to 2 hours in advance, and the salmon kept well chilled.)

2 Toss the slices of avocado in lemon juice to prevent them from dis-colouring.

3 Mix the raspberry vinegar with olive oil, garlic, salt and pepper to taste, and the pink peppercorns.

4 Arrange the salmon and avocado slices, fanned out, on 4 dinner plates; spoon the raspberry vinegar dressing evenly over each portion. Cover loosely with cling film and chill for 30 minutes.

5 Garnish each plate with one or two small tartlets filled with the shredded courgette and topped with a little lumpfish roe, and a sprig of dill.

Cook's Tip The piece of salmon fillet will slice more easily if it is well chilled beforehand.

Variation Try one of the flavoured vinegars, such as mango or kiwi fruit.

The addition of freshly-cooked, split asparagus, fresh dill and oak leaf lettuce makes this dish particularly attractive.

FILLETS OF SOLE WITH MELON AND MINT SAUCE

preparation: 20 minutes

cooking: 10–12 minutes

serves 4

2 small sole, skinned and filleted
(halve each fillet to give 8 pieces)

salt and freshly ground black pepper

2 tablespoons chopped mint

300 ml/½ pint dry white wine

1 Charentais melon, halved and seeded

150 ml/¼ pint thick homemade yogurt
(page 139)

to garnish:

sprigs of fresh mint

1 Season the sole fillets with salt and pepper, and sprinkle with half the mint.
2 Roll up each fish fillet and secure with wooden cocktail sticks. Place the fish rolls in a deep frying pan; sprinkle over the remaining mint and add the white wine.
3 Cover the pan and poach gently for about 8 minutes until the fish is tender.
4 Meanwhile, using a Parisian cutter or melon ball cutter, scoop the melon flesh into small balls. Cut out any remaining melon flesh attached to the skin.
5 Carefully drain the cooked rolled fillets of fish and place on a warm serving dish; keep warm. Remove the cocktail sticks.
6 Boil the poaching liquid with the remnants of melon flesh until well reduced; whisk until smooth. If necessary, blend in a liquidizer or food processor.
7 Stir in the yogurt and heat the sauce through gently. Season with salt and pepper, and spoon over the cooked fish.
8 Garnish with the melon balls and sprigs of mint.

Cook's Tip Be prepared for the addition of the melon to give the sauce a slightly granular texture; do not think that the sauce has curdled.
Variation Other varieties of melon can be used but they do not lend quite the same sweet flavour to the dish as Charentais.

PLAICE ROLLS WITH LETTUCE STUFFING

preparation: 20 minutes

cooking: 18–20 minutes

serves 4

8 small plaice fillets, skinned

finely grated rind of 1 lemon

2 tablespoons chopped parsley

8 anchovy fillets

8 medium cabbage or round lettuce leaves

100 g/4 oz cooked, peeled prawns

salt and freshly ground black pepper

3 spring onions, topped and tailed

15 g/½ oz butter

300 ml/½ pint dry white wine

150 ml/¼ pint Yogurt Mayonnaise
(page 139)

to garnish:

thin slices of lemon

finely chopped parsley

grated lemon rind

1 Lay the plaice fillets skinned side uppermost; sprinkle with lemon rind and parsley and lay an anchovy fillet lengthways along each one.
2 Put a lettuce leaf on top of each plaice fillet, and top with chopped prawns, and salt and pepper to taste. Roll up each one and secure with a wooden cocktail stick.
3 Fry the chopped spring onions gently in the butter for 3 minutes in a large shallow pan; arrange the plaice rolls carefully on top, and add the white wine, and salt and pepper to taste.
4 Cover and poach gently until the rolled plaice fillets are just tender; drain the fish carefully and keep warm.
5 Boil the cooking liquid rapidly until reduced by half; remove from the heat and beat in the Yogurt Mayonnaise. Heat through gently.
6 Arrange the rolled plaice fillets on a warm serving dish, having removed the cocktail sticks. Spoon the sauce evenly over the fish.
7 Sprinkle with a little of the chopped parsley and the grated lemon rind and garnish with the lemon slices sprinkled with the remaning chopped parsley. Serve immediately.

Cook's Tip The fish fillets will roll much more easily if they have not been taken straight from a refrigerator. Tuck the lettuce in as you roll up the fillets to give a neat shape and appearance.
Variation For a very special occasion use slices of smoked salmon in place of the chopped prawns; the plaice fillets can be spread with lumpfish roe and the anchovy fillets omitted.
    As an alternative garnish use the Dry-bake Herb Croûtons (page 140).

Plaice Rolls with Prawn and Lettuce Stuffing: *Rolled fillets of plaice, with a stuffing of lettuce, prawns and anchovy, are served with a light yogurt mayonnaise.*

SOLE AND SMOKED SALMON PAUPIETTES

preparation: 15 minutes

cooking: about 8 minutes

serves 4

8 small sole fillets, skinned

salt and freshly ground black pepper

4 slices smoked salmon (about 100 g/4 oz)

1 tablespoon chopped dill

300 ml/½ pint fish stock (page 137)

300 ml/½ pint Herb and Lemon Sauce
(page 138)

50 g/2 oz cooked, peeled prawns

to garnish:

sprigs of fresh dill

twists of lemon

1 Lay the sole fillets out flat and season with salt and pepper.
2 Cut the slices of smoked salmon in half lengthways and lay a strip down the length of each sole fillet; sprinkle with chopped dill and roll up like a Swiss roll. Secure with wooden cocktail sticks.
3 Place the fish rolls in a shallow pan and add the fish stock; it should half cover the fish. Cover and simmer for about 8 minutes until just tender.
4 Drain the fish and keep warm on a serving dish.
5 Spoon 4 tablespoons of the fish cooking liquid into a small pan; allow to boil quickly over a high heat until reduced to about 1 tablespoon.
6 Stir the Herb and Lemon Sauce and the prawns into the reduced cooking liquid and heat through gently.
7 Spoon the sauce evenly over the fish paupiettes and garnish with sprigs of fresh dill and twists of lemon.

Cook's Tip Do not roll the fish fillets up too tightly, as they tend to contract on cooking and can lose their shape.
Variation Try smoked halibut in place of the smoked salmon.

SALMON AND CRAB MOUSSE

preparation: 40 minutes, plus chilling

serves 4

½ cucumber, thinly sliced

175 g/6 oz cooked salmon, flaked (drained
canned salmon can be used)

100 g/4 oz crabmeat, flaked

150 ml/¼ pint homemade yogurt (page 139)

3 tablespoons dry white wine

2 teaspoons powdered gelatine

finely grated rind of ½ lemon

salt and freshly ground black pepper

2 slices smoked salmon, cut into strips

6 stuffed olives, sliced

1 Grease a 450 g/1 lb loaf tin and line it with non-stick silicone or greased greaseproof paper. Line the base and sides with slices of cucumber, saving some for putting over the top of the mousse.
2 Mix the cooked salmon with the crabmeat and yogurt. Mix the white wine with the gelatine in a small bowl and set aside for 1 minute. Stand the bowl in in a pan of hot water, and leave until the gelatine has dissolved, about 2 minutes.
3 Mix the dissolved gelatine into the fish mixture with the lemon rind and salt and pepper to taste.
4 Spread half the mixture into the loaf tin; lay the smoked salmon strips and the olives on top. Cover with the remaining fish mixture, and then a layer of cucumber.
5 Chill for 4 hours until set.
6 Unmould onto a serving dish and serve cut into slices.

Cook's Tip Do not overlap the sliced cucumber, as the mousse would not then turn out neatly.
Variation Instead of using strips of smoked salmon, you can add peeled prawns.

SEAFOOD SOUFFLE

preparation: 20 minutes

cooking: about 40 minutes

oven temperature: 190°C, 375°F, Gas Mark 5

serves 4

25 g/1 oz butter

40 g/1½ oz wholemeal flour

150 ml/¼ pint skimmed milk

150 ml/¼ pint dry white wine

finely grated rind of ½ lemon

salt and freshly ground black pepper

2 tablespoons finely chopped parsley

4 eggs, separated

175 g/6 oz cooked white fish, flaked

75 g/3 oz flaked crabmeat

50 g/2 oz cooked, peeled prawns, chopped

1 Grease an 18 cm/7 inch soufflé dish.

2 Melt the butter in a pan; stir in the flour and cook for 1 minute. Gradually stir in the skimmed milk and white wine; bring to the boil, stirring, and simmer until the sauce has thickened.

3 Beat in the lemon rind, salt and pepper to taste, parsley, and egg yolks; mix in the fish, crabmeat and prawns.

4 Whisk the egg whites until stiff but not dry; fold lightly but thoroughly into the fish sauce.

5 Transfer the mixture to the prepared soufflé dish. Bake in the preheated oven for about 35 minutes, until well risen, puffed and golden.

6 Serve immediately.

Cook's Tip Take care not to overbeat the egg whites; if you do so, the soufflé mixture will be speckled with unmixed patches of egg white.

Variation Try using the same amount of smoked mackerel or salmon in place of the white fish and shellfish.

SPATCHCOCK MEDITERRANEAN PRAWNS

preparation: 20 minutes, plus chilling

cooking: 3 minutes

serves 4

12–16 raw Mediterranean prawns,

4 tablespoons olive oil

finely grated rind and juice of 1 lemon

2 garlic cloves, peeled and finely chopped

1 teaspoon chopped thyme

1 teaspoon chopped feathery fennel, or dill

vine leaves

to garnish:

wedges of lemon

1 Split each prawn lengthways along its underside, from head to tail, without cutting completely through the back shell. Carefully open each prawn out flat, and thread a small metal skewer or wooden cocktail stick through each one, to hold it open.

2 Place the prawns, cut side uppermost, in a shallow ovenproof dish in a single layer.

3 Mix the olive oil with the lemon rind and juice, garlic, herbs, and salt and pepper to taste; spoon evenly over the prawns.

4 Cover the dish and chill for at least 4 hours, or preferably overnight.

5 Lift the prawns out of their marinade and place on the rack of the grill pan, cut surfaces uppermost; spoon over some of the marinade.

6 Grill the prawns for 2–3 minutes.

7 Arrange the prawns on a bed of vine leaves and garnish with wedges of lemon. Serve accompanied by a bowl of Yogurt Mayonnaise (page 139).

Cook's Tip The simplest way of splitting the prawns is to use a pair of small scissors with slim blades.

Variation Freshwater crayfish can be treated in exactly the same way.

ANTIBES SAFFRON STEW

preparation: 25 minutes

cooking: 40 minutes

serves 4

½ teaspoon saffron strands

1 large onion, peeled and finely chopped

2 tablespoons olive oil

2 garlic cloves, peeled and finely chopped

2 tablespoons coarsely chopped parsley

1 tablespoon chopped thyme

600 ml/1 pint fish stock (page 137)

300 ml/½ pint dry white wine

6 large tomatoes, skinned and seeded

350 g/12 oz monkfish, cubed

350 g/12 oz cleaned squid, cut into rings

16 fresh mussels, scrubbed

8 raw Mediterranean prawns, headed

salt and freshly ground black pepper

croûtes:

8 thin slices wholemeal French bread

1 tablespoon olive oil

1 large garlic clove, peeled and crushed

2 tablespoons grated Parmesan cheese

1 Soak the saffron in 4 tablespoons of boiling water. Fry the onion gently in the olive oil with the garlic for 3 minutes; add the herbs and fry gently for a further 3 minutes.
2 Add the stock and white wine; bring to the boil and simmer for 10 minutes. Add the chopped tomatoes and strained saffron liquid and simmer for 5 minutes.
3 Add the monkfish and the squid and simmer for 10 minutes.
4 Add the mussels and Mediterranean prawns, and season to taste with salt and pepper; simmer for a further 5–6 minutes.
5 Meanwhile prepare the croûtes: toast the slices of French bread on one side only. Brush the untoasted side with the olive oil and sprinkle with the garlic and Parmesan cheese. Place under a moderately hot grill until golden.
6 Place two hot croûtes into the bottom of four deep soup bowls and ladle on the hot fish stew. Serve immediately.

Cook's Tip Remember to check the mussels carefully prior to cooking. Any broken or damaged shells should be discarded.
Variation The cooking liquid from the stew can be thickened. Remove the cooked fish with a slotted spoon and keep warm. Beat 3 egg yolks with 4 tablespoons crème fraîche and whisk into the hot cooking liquid; stir over a gentle heat until thickened. Return the fish and warm through briefly.

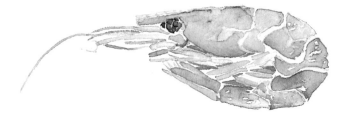

BAKED CHEESY CRAB

preparation: 20 minutes

cooking: about 15 minutes

oven temperature: 190°C, 375°F, Gas Mark 5

serves 4

450 g/1 lb white crabmeat

150 ml/¼ pint Yogurt Mayonnaise (page 139)

salt and freshly ground black pepper

few drops of Tabasco

2 hard-boiled eggs

100 g/4 oz Edam or Gouda cheese, grated

2 tablespoons wholemeal breadcrumbs

1 Mix the crabmeat with the Yogurt Mayonnaise, salt and pepper to taste and Tabasco.
2 Separate the yolks and whites from the hard-boiled eggs; chop the whites and sieve the yolks.
3 Stir the egg whites and half the cheese into the crab mixture; divide between four individual greased gratin dishes.
4 Sprinkle with the breadcrumbs, egg yolk and the remaining cheese.
5 Place in the preheated oven and bake for about 15 minutes until the tops are golden.
6 Serve piping hot.

Cook's Tip Always check crabmeat very carefully to make sure that it contains no pieces of loose shell.
Variation This recipe is also very good prepared with freshly cooked and flaked salmon; use a tail piece as it is less expensive.

Antibes Stew: *An unforgettable taste for the shellfish lover: rings of squid,*
succulent Mediterranean prawns and mussels are bathed in a
saffron and wine sauce

SCALLOP LOAF WITH PIMENTO SAUCE

preparation: 45 minutes, plus chilling

cooking: 20−25 minutes

serves 4−6

750 g/1½ lb haddock fillet

600 ml/1 pint fish stock (page 137)

1 tablespoon white wine vinegar

juice of ½ lemon

6 shelled large scallops

100 g/4 oz French beans, topped and tailed

225 g/8 oz carrots, peeled and cut into

5 mm/¼ inch strips

15 g/½ oz powdered gelatine

3 tablespoons water

6 medium fresh asparagus tips, cooked

sauce:

1 large red pepper, cored, seeded and chopped

150 ml/¼ pint dry white wine

150 ml/¼ pint chicken stock (page 137)

1 garlic clove, peeled and crushed

salt and freshly ground black pepper

1 Grease and line a 900 g/2 lb loaf tin with non-stick silicone or greased greaseproof paper.

2 Put the haddock fillet into a pan with the stock, wine vinegar and lemon juice; poach gently for 5−6 minutes until the haddock is just tender. Drain the fish, reserving the cooking liquid.

3 Remove the coral from each scallop and cut the scallops into slices; poach gently in the reserved cooking liquid for 5−6 minutes. Drain the scallops, and strain the cooking liquid.

4 Blanch the beans and carrots separately in boiling salted water, and then refresh in very cold water. Drain thoroughly.

5 Put the gelatine and water into a small bowl and set aside for 1 minute. Stand the bowl in a pan of hot water and leave until the gelatine has dissolved, about 2 minutes. Stir the dissolved gelatine into the strained cooking liquid and leave on one side, until syrupy.

6 Skin and flake the haddock. Divide the haddock, coral and sliced scallops into four equal portions. Put one portion into the prepared loaf tin; top with the beans. Add a further portion of the fish mixture and top with the carrots. Add another portion of the fish and then top with the asparagus tips. Add the final portion of fish mixture.

7 Pour in the syrupy cooking liquid. Chill for 4−6 hours until set.

8 Meanwhile make the sauce: put the red pepper, white wine, stock, garlic, and salt and pepper to taste into a pan; simmer until the red pepper is soft. Place the sauce in a liquidizer or food processor; blend until smooth. Chill.

9 Serve the scallop loaf in slices, with a little of the pimento sauce.

Cook's Tip The scallop loaf will slice even more easily if it is made the day before and chilled overnight. If it proves a little difficult to turn out, dip the base of the tin briefly in hot water. Flower heads cut from rings of carrot, tiny florets of blanched broccoli, and petals cut from tomato make an attractive garnish arranged around each portion.

Variation Alternatively, serve the sliced loaf with Herb and Lemon Sauce (page 138) and garnish with cooked asparagus tips, strips of orange rind and snipped chives.

MUSSEL AND WINE CASSEROLE

preparation: 10 minutes

cooking: about 10 minutes

serves 4

300 ml/½ pint Tomato Sauce (page 138)

200 ml/⅓ pint red wine

2 garlic cloves, peeled and chopped

3 tablespoons chopped parsley

salt and freshly ground black pepper

2.25 litres/4 pints mussels, scrubbed

Dry-bake Herb Croûtons (page 140)

1 Put the Tomato Sauce into a deep pan with the red wine, garlic, parsley, and salt and pepper to taste; bring to the boil and simmer gently for 5 minutes.

2 Add the mussels, cover the pan, and continue simmering for 4−5 minutes; give the pan a good shake once or twice during this time.

3 Put two or three croûtons into the bottom of four deep soup bowls and ladle the hot mussels and their sauce on top, discarding any mussels which have not fully opened.

4 Serve piping hot.

Cook's Tip It is essential to check the mussels very carefully before cooking and discard any that have broken or damaged shells.

Variation For a lighter-flavoured sauce, cook the mussels in about 450 ml/¾ pint dry white wine – in place of the Tomato Sauce and red wine – with the garlic, parsley, salt and pepper.

Scallop Loaf: *A delicious wine and fish jelly sets tender scallops, asparagus tips, green beans and carrots in an attractive seafood loaf.*

Meat & Poultry

Our ancestors consumed meat in alarmingly large quantities. In medieval times, they would hack at whole animals turning on open spits. What we would consider a Sunday joint would have been served as a single portion to a nobleman! They gave no thought to whether such a diet was good for them, but ate lustily with apparent enjoyment.

Now our tastes are changing and we are eating smaller, more realistic portions, and favouring the less fatty foods such as veal, chicken, turkey and fish. The lower-than-usual proportion of meat to other ingredients in *Lean Cuisine* recipes is also indicative of this trend.

It took many years for us to realize that a meal does not necessarily have to include meat to be satisfying. Equally, even when we do choose meat, game or poultry, such foods do not have to be served hot. Served cold, they are just as nourishing, and the flavour is often more intense, especially if the raw meat has been marinated before cooking. If you want to cook meat specifically to serve it cold, poaching is one of the best methods as the meat will remain moist.

The sauces really make many of these recipes, combining some unusual flavours and textures — for example, several fresh fruit-based sauces, such as those used in Chicken with Fresh Mango Sauce and Lamb Reine Claude. I have also created some lovely, creamy-textured sauces, using yogurt or fromage blanc, which are much lower in fat than the cream-based varieties. Herbs, green peppercorns, saffron and capers all help to enhance the natural flavours, and give that special individual touch to the respective dishes.

Eating meat and poultry the *Lean Cuisine* way means enjoying some outstanding main course dishes. I think that our ancestors might have been a little envious of us!

RAW BEEF WITH MUSTARD AND GHERKINS

preparation: 25 minutes

serves 4

3 tablespoons homemade yogurt (page 137)

2 teaspoons coarse grain mustard

1 tablespoon chopped chives

1 garlic clove, peeled and crushed

1 tablespoon dry sherry

salt and freshly ground black pepper

450 g/1 lb fillet of beef, in one piece

2 tablespoons virgin olive oil

2 tablespoons finely chopped gherkin

thin strips of spring onion

to garnish:

thin slices of cucumber

sprigs of fresh basil

gherkin fans

1 Mix the yogurt with the mustard, chives, garlic, sherry, and salt and pepper to taste.
2 Using a very sharp knife, cut the beef into paper-thin slices (see Cook's Tip). Arrange them overlapping on four dinner plates.
3 Trickle a little olive oil over each portion; add a little gherkin and thin strips of spring onion to each portion.
4 Garnish each one with 3 slices of cucumber topped with a little of the prepared sauce, a sprig of fresh basil and a gherkin fan.

Cook's Tip The fillet of beef is much easier to slice if it is well chilled beforehand; you can even put it into the freezer for 30 minutes. Serve the beef as soon as possible after slicing, as it darkens very quickly.
Variation Serve the sliced raw beef with a fruit purée rather than the mustard and yogurt dressing suggested above; choose one that is quite sharp, such as apricot or raspberry.

WHITE LAMB CASSEROLE

preparation: 10 minutes

cooking: about 1 hour 10 minutes

oven temperature: 180°C, 350°F, Gas Mark 4

serves 4

2 medium onions, peeled and thinly sliced

1 tablespoon olive oil

1 garlic clove, peeled and crushed

450 g/1 lb lean lamb, cut into small cubes

1 × 425 g/15 oz can chick peas, rinsed and drained

400 ml/14 fl oz pint chicken stock (page 137)

1 teaspoon saffron strands, soaked in

2 tablespoons boiling water

salt and freshly ground black pepper

2 tablespoons homemade yogurt

(page 139)

1 Fry the onions gently in the oil in a non-stick pan for 3 minutes; add the garlic and lamb and cook until the meat is evenly coloured on all sides.
2 Transfer the lamb and onions to a casserole and add half the drained chick peas.
3 Put the remaining chick peas into a liquidizer or food processor with the chicken stock, strained saffron liquid, and salt and pepper to taste; blend until smooth.
4 Pour the blended sauce into the casserole. Cover and cook in the preheated oven for about 1 hour, or until the lamb is tender.
5 Swirl the yogurt over the top and serve immediately.

Cook's Tip The total cooking time will depend on the cut of lamb: fillet will cook in 1 hour, whereas boned leg meat may take a little longer.
Variation Red kidney beans can be used in place of chick peas, but they will naturally change the colour of the casserole. Use canned ones, or well-cooked dried ones.

Raw Beef with Mustard and Gherkins: *Wafer thin slices of raw beef beautifully garnished with gherkin, sliced cucumber, shreds of spring onion and basil leaves.*

LAMB REINE CLAUDE

preparation: 10 minutes

cooking: 25—30 minutes

serves 4

450 g/1 lb Reine Claude plums, or
greengages, halved and stoned

150 ml/¼ pint chicken stock (page 139)

3 tablespoons Crème de Cassis

450 g/1 lb lamb fillet, cut into small
medallions

2 tablespoons olive oil

salt and freshly ground black pepper

1 Put the plums or greengages into a pan with the chicken stock and simmer gently for 5 minutes.
2 Put the plums and their liquid into a liquidizer or food processor with the Crème de Cassis; blend to a smooth purée.
3 Fry the lamb medallions in the olive oil until evenly browned on all sides; add the plum and Cassis purée and season to taste with salt and pepper.
4 Cover and simmer for about 15—20 minutes until the lamb is quite tender.
5 Serve immediately.

Cook's Tip If you are going to sieve the plum sauce, rather than blend it, there is no need to stone the plums in advance.
Variation This recipe is just as delicious if the sauce is prepared with fresh apricots; but it is better to blanch and skin them before cooking.

CALVES' LIVER FLORENTINE

preparation: about 10 minutes

cooking: 8—10 minutes

serves 4

750 g/1½ lb fresh spinach, cooked and
drained

freshly ground nutmeg

salt and freshly ground black pepper

450 g/1 lb calves' liver, cut into thin slices

15 g/½ oz butter

2 tablespoons olive oil

1 tablespoon chopped sage

1 garlic clove, peeled and crushed

150 ml/¼ pint homemade yogurt (page 139)

1 egg yolk

50 g/2 oz Edam or Gouda cheese, grated

1 Season the spinach with nutmeg, salt and pepper; spoon into a lightly greased flameproof dish.
2 Fry the slices of liver gently in the butter and oil, together with the sage and garlic, until sealed on all sides.
3 Spoon the liver and its juices over the spinach.
4 Beat the yogurt with the egg yolk and spoon evenly over the liver and spinach; sprinkle with the cheese.
5 Place under a preheated grill until the sauce is lightly golden and bubbling.
6 Serve immediately.

Cook's Tip Make sure that the cooked spinach is drained thoroughly, otherwise the finished dish will be far too liquid.
Variation Try using the same quantity of fried chicken livers in place of the sliced calves' liver.

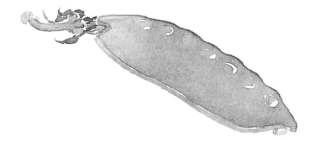

MARINATED KIDNEYS

preparation: 15 minutes, plus chilling

cooking: about 8 minutes

serves 4

12 lambs' kidneys, skinned, cored and halved

1 small onion, peeled and thinly sliced

1 garlic clove, peeled and finely chopped

salt and freshly ground black pepper

150 ml/¼ pint red wine

1 teaspoon chopped fresh thyme

1 teaspoon French mustard

2 tablespoons Basil and Garlic Oil (page 138)

1 Put the kidneys into a shallow dish; add the onion, garlic, salt and pepper to taste, red wine, thyme and mustard. Cover and chill for 3–4 hours.
2 Lift the kidneys out of their marinade and thread flat onto four kebab skewers.
3 Brush the kidneys with the Basil and Garlic Oil and grill for 3 minutes; turn the skewers over, brush once again, and grill for a further 3 minutes.
4 Heat the marinade until boiling. Arrange the kebabs on a serving dish, spoon over the hot marinade and serve immediately.

Cook's Tip The simplest way of removing the cores from kidneys is to snip them out with scissors.
Variation Try using a medium sherry for the marinade instead of red wine.

LEMON VEAL CASSEROLE

preparation: 15 minutes, plus chilling

cooking: about 1¼ hours

oven temperature: 180°C, 350°F, Gas Mark 4

serves 4

500 g/1¼ lb lean veal, cut into 2 cm/¾ inch cubes

finely grated rind and juice of 1 lemon

1 tablespoon chopped coriander

salt and freshly ground black pepper

1 garlic clove, peeled and crushed

2 tablespoons olive oil

300 ml/½ pint chicken stock (page 137)

150 ml/¼ pint dry white wine

3 courgettes, topped, tailed and cut into strips

100 g/4 oz shelled broad beans (fresh or frozen)

3 tablespoons fromage blanc (page 140)

1 Put the veal into a shallow dish with the lemon rind and juice, coriander, and salt and pepper to taste; cover and chill for 3–4 hours.
2 Drain the veal and reserve the marinade. Fry the garlic in the oil for 30 seconds; add the veal and fry until evenly browned.
3 Put the veal and the reserved marinade into a casserole with the stock, white wine, courgettes and broad beans. Cover the casserole and cook in the preheated oven for about 1 hour until the veal is tender.
4 Stir in the fromage blanc and return to the oven for a further 5 minutes.
5 Serve piping hot with green fettucine (page 103).

Cook's Tip If you blend the fromage blanc with a little of the hot cooking liquid before adding it to the casserole, it will blend in more readily.
Variation The lemon gives a very tangy taste; for a less tart flavour, substitute an orange for the lemon.

VEAL AND PEPPER STIR-FRY

preparation: 5 minutes

cooking: 11–12 minutes

serves 4

1 medium onion, peeled and thinly sliced

3 tablespoons olive oil

450 g/1 lb veal fillet, cut into thin strips

1 red pepper, cored, seeded and cut into thin strips

1 green pepper, cored, seeded and cut into thin strips

2 garlic cloves, peeled and chopped

2 tablespoons cashew nuts

1 tablespoon soy sauce

1 tablespoon oyster sauce

2 tablespoons dry sherry

freshly ground black pepper

1 Fry the onion gently in the oil, either in a wok or a deep frying pan, for about 3 minutes.

2 Add the veal fillet strips and stir-fry until evenly sealed on all sides.

3 Add the pepper strips, garlic and cashew nuts, and stir-fry for 3 minutes.

4 Add the remaining ingredients with pepper to taste, and stir-fry for a further 2–3 minutes. Serve piping hot.

Cook's Tip Ingredients for stir-frying need to be cut really finely; they then cook very quickly without losing their texture, colour or flavour.

Variation Thin strips of skinned chicken or turkey breast can be used in place of the veal.

VEAL MEDALLIONS WITH RED WINE VINEGAR SAUCE

preparation: 8–10 minutes

cooking: about 15 minutes

serves 4

25 g/1 oz butter

1 small onion, peeled and finely chopped

1 garlic clove, peeled and finely chopped

4 tablespoons red wine vinegar

300 ml/½ pint chicken stock (page 137)

salt and freshly ground black pepper

4 veal medallions

1 tablespoon chopped fresh rosemary

100 g/4 oz fresh or frozen redcurrants

to garnish:

leaf-shaped croûtons spread with pesto sauce

sprigs of rosemary

1 Melt half the butter; add the onion and garlic and fry gently for 3 minutes.

2 Add the red wine vinegar, stock, and salt and pepper to taste; simmer gently for 5 minutes.

3 Meanwhile heat the remaining butter in a shallow frying pan; add the veal medallions and fry until sealed on both sides.

4 Add the rosemary and the red wine vinegar sauce; add the redcurrants and simmer for 4–5 minutes.

5 Garnish with small leaf-shaped croûtons spread with pesto sauce and a sprig of rosemary.

Cook's Tip If preferred, the veal medallions can be sealed on both sides as in the recipe and then put into an ovenproof dish with the sauce ingredients; cook, covered, for 30 minutes in a preheated oven, 190°C/375°F/Gas Mark 5.

Variation Pork fillets cut into medallions can be used in place of veal. A little honey can be added to the sauce to make it less sharp.

Veal Medallions with Red Wine Vinegar Sauce: *Thin steaks of*
veal cooked in a soft wine vinegar sauce, garnished with redcurrants,
leaf-shaped croûtons and rosemary.

RABBIT WITH ROSEMARY AND MUSTARD

preparation: about 10 minutes

cooking: about 55 minutes

serves 4

1 medium onion, peeled and finely
chopped

2 tablespoons olive oil

4 rabbit joints (about 200 g/7 oz each)

300 ml/½ pint chicken stock (page 137)

200 ml/⅓ pint dry white wine

2 teaspoons coarse grain mustard

1 tablespoon chopped rosemary

salt and freshly ground black pepper

3 tablespoons fromage blanc (page 140)

2 egg yolks

to garnish:

sprigs of fresh rosemary

1 Fry the onion gently in the olive oil for 3 minutes; add the rabbit joints and brown evenly on all sides.
2 Add the chicken stock, white wine, mustard, rosemary, and salt and pepper to taste; cover and simmer for 45 minutes until the rabbit is just tender.
3 Remove the rabbit joints to a serving dish and keep warm.
4 Boil the cooking liquid rapidly until reduced by half; beat the fromage blanc with the egg yolks and whisk into the cooking liquid over a gentle heat, without boiling.
5 Spoon the prepared sauce over the rabbit and garnish with sprigs of fresh rosemary.

Cook's Tip If you are using frozen rabbit, make sure that the joints are completely thawed before cooking.
Variation Other mustards can be used but they will not give quite the same pungency and texture as a coarse grain mustard.

PORK FILLET WITH GRAPEFRUIT SAUCE

preparation: 15 minutes, plus chilling

cooking: about 10 minutes

serves 4

450 g/1 lb pork fillet, cut into 5 mm/¼ inch
thick medallions

3 spring onions, topped, tailed and finely
chopped

finely grated rind and juice of ½ grapefruit

1 teaspoon soft brown sugar

salt and freshly ground black pepper

2 tablespoons chopped parsley

2 tablespoons olive oil

150 ml/¼ pint unsweetened apple purée

150 ml/¼ pint chicken stock (page 137)

peeled segments from 2 grapefruit

1 Marinate the pork medallions with the spring onions, grapefruit rind and juice, brown sugar, salt and pepper to taste, and the parsley. Cover and chill for 3–4 hours.
2 Drain the pork medallions, reserving the marinade.
3 Fry the medallions briskly in the oil until sealed on all sides.
4 Mix the apple purée with the stock and marinade and pour over the pork; cover and simmer for about 7 minutes until the pork is tender.
5 Stir in the grapefruit segments and heat through.

Cook's Tip Cut a thin slice from both ends of the grapefruit, stand the grapefruit on one cut surface on a chopping board and with a sharp knife cut down from the top to the bottom in a curved motion, following the shape of the fruit. When the peel has been completely removed, cut between the membrane to loosen each segment.
Variation Other unsweetened fruit purées such as apricot or pear can be used instead of apple.

POACHED GUINEA FOWL WITH CHEESE STUFFING

preparation: 30 minutes

cooking: about 1 hour

serves 4

1 guinea fowl (about 1.25 kg/2½ lb),
prepared for cooking

75 g/3 oz curd cheese

3 garlic cloves, peeled and crushed

1 tablespoon chopped basil

1 tablespoon chopped tarragon

salt and freshly ground black pepper

300 ml/½ pint chicken stock (page 137)

300 ml/½ pint dry white wine

sauce:

3 tablespoons chopped basil

4 tablespoons olive oil

2 egg yolks

2 tablespoons pine kernels

1 Insert your fingers carefully between the skin and flesh at the neck end of the bird. Then run your fingers carefully along the length of the breast of the bird to separate the skin from the flesh, taking great care not to puncture the skin with your nails.
2 Mix the curd cheese with the garlic, basil, tarragon, and salt and pepper to taste; ease the cheese mixture between the skin and flesh of the guinea fowl. Ease the skin back into shape over the bird.
3 Put the prepared guinea fowl into a large pan and add the stock and white wine; cover and simmer gently for 1 hour, until the guinea fowl is just tender.
4 Lift the guinea fowl onto a warmed serving dish and keep warm. Reserve the cooking liquid.
5 To make the sauce, put the basil, olive oil, egg yolks and pine kernels into a liquidizer or food processor; blend until smooth. Gradually blend in 200 ml/⅓ pint of the cooking liquid. Heat the sauce through gently in a small pan.
6 Carve the guinea fowl into portions and serve accompanied by the sauce.

Cook's Tip Choose good, plump guinea fowl for this recipe. You will find it easier to stuff the guinea fowl with the cheese mixture if the bird has not come straight from the refrigerator.
Variation You can use a small chicken in place of the guinea fowl, if preferred.

POACHED CHICKEN BREASTS WITH SPRING VEGETABLES

preparation: 15 minutes

cooking: 35—40 minutes

serves 4

6 small courgettes, topped, tailed and
sliced lengthways

100 g/4 oz baby carrots, scraped

100 g/4 oz shelled broad beans

2 garlic cloves, peeled and finely chopped

1 tablespoon chopped chives

4 chicken breasts, skinned and boned

300 ml/½ pint chicken stock (page 137)

1 bunch watercress, washed and trimmed

1 teaspoon pesto sauce

salt and freshly ground black pepper

1 Lay the courgettes, baby carrots and broad beans in the base of a deep frying pan; sprinkle with the garlic and the chives.
2 Lay the chicken breasts on the top.
3 Put the chicken stock, watercress, pesto sauce, and salt and pepper to taste into a liquidizer or food processor; blend until smooth.
4 Pour the watercress sauce over the chicken and vegetables; cover and simmer gently for about 35—40 minutes until the chicken and vegetables are tender.
5 Serve immediately.

Cook's Tip Use really fresh young vegetables for maximum flavour.
Variation Thin veal medallions cut from the fillet can be used in place of the chicken breasts; allow roughly the same cooking time.

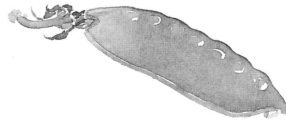

BABY CHICKENS WITH OLIVES

preparation: 20 minutes

cooking: about 1 hour

oven temperature: 180°C, 350°F, Gas Mark 4

serves 4

4 baby chickens (poussins)

1 orange, cut into chunks

2 garlic cloves, peeled and split in half

handful of parsley

3 celery sticks, chopped

2 medium carrots, peeled and sliced

100 g/4 oz stoned green olives

salt and freshly ground black pepper

750 ml/1¼ pints chicken stock (page 137)

1 Ease the cavity of each baby chicken open; tuck a few orange chunks, half a garlic clove and a few sprigs of parsley into each one. Secure the opening with a wooden cocktail stick.
2 Put the prepared baby chickens into a large casserole; add the celery, carrots, half the green olives, salt and pepper to taste, and the stock. Cover the casserole and cook in the preheated oven for about 1 hour, or until the chickens are tender.
3 Lift the baby chickens onto a warm serving dish, remove the cocktail sticks and keep warm. Place the cooking juices, vegetables and olives in a food processor or liquidizer; blend until smooth. Add the remaining olives and heat through gently in a pan.
4 Spoon the olive sauce over the baby chickens and serve immediately.

Cook's Tip Baby chickens are often not plucked as well as the larger birds; go over them carefully and remove any stray feathers or stubbly pieces.
Variation Chicken leg joints can be used instead of baby chickens.

TURKEY AND PARMA HAM KEBABS

preparation: 20 minutes, plus chilling

cooking: about 10 minutes

serves 4

450 g/1 lb turkey fillet, cut into

4 cm/1½ inch cubes

grated rind of 1 lemon

1 small onion, peeled and finely chopped

1 garlic clove, peeled and finely chopped

1 teaspoon pesto sauce

3 tablespoons Basil and Garlic Oil (page 138)

salt and freshly ground black pepper

100 g/4 oz Parma ham, cut into long strips

8 small button mushrooms

8 small bay leaves

8 wedges of lemon

shredded lettuce

1 Put the turkey fillet into a shallow dish. Mix the lemon rind with the onion, garlic, pesto sauce, Basil and Garlic Oil, and salt and pepper to taste.
2 Stir the marinade into the turkey; cover and chill for 3−4 hours.
3 Drain the turkey, reserving the marinade. Wrap each piece of turkey in a strip of Parma ham.
4 Thread the turkey and ham rolls onto kebab skewers, alternating with the mushrooms, bay leaves and wedges of lemon.
5 Brush the threaded skewers with the marinade; grill for 4−5 minutes. Turn the kebab skewers, brush once again with the marinade, and grill for a further 4−5 minutes.
6 Serve piping hot on a bed of shredded lettuce.

Cook's Tip The ham will wrap round the turkey more easily if it is moist. It is important, therefore, to keep it closely covered in the refrigerator so that it does not dry out.
Variation Chicken breast fillet can be used instead of turkey, and lean ham can be substituted for Parma ham.

Turkey and Parma Ham Kebabs: *Lean cubes of turkey wrapped in
Parma Ham and skewered with bay leaves, wedges of lemon
and small mushrooms.*

89

TURKEY TROT WITH TUNA

preparation: 10 minutes

cooking: about 50 minutes

serves 4

2 turkey thighs

600 ml/1 pint chicken stock (page 137)

2 bay leaves

sprig of rosemary

sprig of sage

salt and freshly ground black pepper

1 large garlic clove, peeled and crushed

1 × 200 g/7 oz can tuna fish in brine, drained

3 anchovy fillets

2 teaspoons capers

300 ml/½ pint Yogurt Mayonnaise (page 139)

grated rind and juice of ½ lemon

to garnish:

extra capers

fresh sage leaves

1 Put the turkey thighs into a pan with the chicken stock, bay leaves, rosemary, sage, salt and pepper to taste, and the garlic; cover and simmer gently for about 50 minutes until the turkey is tender.
2 Meanwhile put the drained tuna fish into a liquidizer or food processor with the anchovy fillets, capers, Yogurt Mayonnaise and lemon rind and juice; blend until smooth.
3 Put the tuna fish sauce into the top of a double saucepan, season to taste with salt and pepper, and heat through gently.
4 Remove the cooked turkey thighs from the pan and carve off the meat as neatly as possible.
5 Arrange the turkey meat on a warm serving dish and spoon over the prepared sauce. Garnish with capers and sage leaves and serve immediately.

Cook's Tip If the tuna sauce seems too thick, add a little of the cooking liquid from the turkey.
Variation Canned salmon makes a pleasant sauce for the turkey instead of tuna.

CHICKEN WITH FRESH MANGO SAUCE

preparation: 25 minutes

cooking: about 15 minutes

serves 4

1 large ripe mango (see Cook's Tip)

200 ml/⅓ pint chicken stock

3 tablespoons dry white wine

juice of ½ lemon

4 chicken breasts, skinned and boned

25 g/1 oz butter

salt and freshly ground black pepper

1 teaspoon pink peppercorns

2 tablespoons homemade yogurt (page 139)

1 Halve the mango and remove the stone carefully; cut eight thin slices from the better-looking half of the mango. Scoop all the flesh from the remaining mango.
2 Put the mango flesh into a liquidizer or food processor with the chicken stock, white wine and lemon juice; blend until smooth.
3 Fry the chicken breasts in the butter until evenly browned on all sides; add salt and pepper to taste and the mango sauce, and simmer, covered, for about 8 minutes.
4 Stir in the pink peppercorns and the yogurt, and heat through.
5 Arrange on a warm serving dish and garnish with the slices of mango.

Cook's Tip The stone runs lengthways through the mango; insert the tip of a small knife at one or two points to find out which way the stone is running. Insert a sharp knife at one end of the mango and cut through, keeping the blade of the knife as close to the stone as possible. Repeat with the other half of the mango to remove the stone completely.
Variation Two fresh peaches can be used instead of the mango.

CHICKEN OLIVES WITH ORANGE AND NUT STUFFING

preparation: 20 minutes

cooking: 30—35 minutes

serves 4

4 chicken breasts, skinned, boned, and
flattened out (see Cook's Tip)

finely grated rind of 1 orange

4 tablespoons fresh wholemeal
breadcrumbs

1 small onion, peeled and finely chopped

salt and freshly ground black pepper

1 tablespoon chopped rosemary

2 tablespoons chopped walnuts

1 egg, beaten

150 ml/¼ pint chicken stock (page 137)

150 ml/¼ pint fresh orange juice

to garnish:

sprigs of fresh rosemary

peeled orange segments

1 Lay the chicken breasts out flat and trim off any uneven edges.

2 Mix the orange rind with the breadcrumbs, onion, salt and pepper to taste, rosemary and walnuts, and bind together with the beaten egg.

3 Spread the stuffing mixture evenly over each chicken breast; roll up securely as for a beef olive. Tie with strong cotton or fine string.

4 Put the chicken olives into a shallow pan and add the chicken stock and orange juice; cover, bring to the boil and simmer for 25—30 minutes, until the chicken is just tender.

5 Remove the chicken olives and keep warm on a serving dish. Boil the cooking liquid until reduced by half.

6 Spoon the cooking liquid over the chicken olives and garnish with rosemary sprigs and orange segments.

Cook's Tip If you need to flatten the chicken breasts yourself, place them between dampened sheets of greaseproof paper and beat with a meat mallet or rolling pin.

Variation Turkey breasts can also be prepared in exactly the same way.

CHICKEN AND TARRAGON LOAF

preparation: 10—15 minutes

cooking: 1¼ hours

oven temperature: 180°C, 350°F, Gas Mark 4

serves 4

450 g/1 lb minced lean chicken

100 g/4 oz minced lean ham

1 small onion, peeled and very
finely chopped

1½ tablespoons chopped tarragon

50 g/2 oz fresh wholemeal breadcrumbs

1 egg, beaten

salt and freshly ground black pepper

3 tablespoons dry vermouth

1 Grease and line a 450 g/1 lb loaf tin with non-stick silicone or greased greaseproof paper.

2 Mix the chicken with the ham, onion, tarragon, breadcrumbs, beaten egg, salt and pepper to taste, and the dry vermouth. Press the mixture into the prepared tin.

3 Stand the tin in a large roasting tin and add hot water to come halfway up the sides of the loaf tin; cover the loaf tin with a piece of greased foil.

4 Cook in the preheated oven for 1¼ hours.

5 Allow to cool in the tin for a few minutes; unmould carefully onto a warm serving dish.

6 Serve, cut into slices, with Yogurt Mayonnaise (page 139).

Cook's Tip If you want to serve the loaf cold, weight it down slightly when it is taken out of the oven.

Variation This loaf is also very good served with Tomato Sauce (page 138).

SMOKED CHICKEN WITH RHUBARB SAUCE

preparation: 10 minutes

cooking: 15 minutes

serves 4

350 g/12 oz rhubarb, trimmed and chopped

grated rind and juice of 1 orange

1 thin slice fresh root ginger, chopped

salt and freshly ground black pepper

200 ml/⅓ pint dry white wine

200 ml/⅓ pint chicken stock (page 137)

2 tablespoons redcurrant jelly

pink food colouring (optional)

350 g/12 oz boned smoked chicken, cut

into thin slices

to garnish:

shredded radicchio

poached strips of young rhubarb

small bay leaves

1 Put the rhubarb into a pan with the orange rind and juice, ginger, salt and pepper to taste, white wine and chicken stock; simmer, covered, for 10 minutes.

2 Blend the sauce in a liquidizer or food processor until smooth; return to a saucepan, add the redcurrant jelly, and stir over a gentle heat until dissolved.

3 Tint the sauce with a little food colouring if liked. Add the pieces of smoked chicken and heat through gently.

4 Arrange on a serving platter with a border of radicchio, and garnish with rhubarb and bay leaves.

Cook's Tip You need a really sharp knife with a slim blade to cut smoked chicken successfully; remove the legs before you try to cut the breast meat.

Variation To make the sauce creamy, stir into it a few tablespoons of homemade yogurt (page 139) blended with an egg yolk.

DUCK WITH PEACH AND GREEN PEPPERCORN SAUCE

preparation: 10 minutes

cooking: 12–15 minutes

serves 4

2 large ripe peaches, blanched, halved,

stoned and skinned

400 ml/14 fl oz dry white wine

4 duck breasts, skinned

15 g/½ oz butter

salt and freshly ground black pepper

1 teaspoon green peppercorns

1 tablespoon chopped basil

to garnish:

slices of fresh ripe peach (including skin)

sprigs of fresh basil

1 Put the blanched halved peaches into a liquidizer or food processor with half the white wine; blend to a smooth purée.

2 Fry the duck breasts in the butter in a non-stick pan until sealed on both sides; add salt and pepper to taste, the green peppercorns, basil and remaining wine. Simmer steadily for 5 minutes.

3 Stir in the peach purée and simmer for a further 4–5 minutes. Ideally the duck breasts should still be quite pink in the centre; if you do not like duck cooked so lightly, simmer it in the sauce for longer.

4 Make four long cuts in each cooked duck breast so that they can be fanned out; arrange them in this manner on four dinner plates.

5 Spoon the warm peach sauce around the duck and garnish with slices of peach and sprigs of basil.

Cook's Tip Duck breasts are not always easy to buy ready-prepared, but it is worth buying two small whole ducks, cutting off the breasts and using the remainder of the birds for a pâté, terrine or soup.

Variation Four fresh apricots can be used as the base for the sauce instead of the peaches.

Duck with Peach and Green Peppercorn Sauce: *A fan of lightly cooked duck served with a fresh fruit sauce; a delightful accompaniment to offset the richness of the duck.*

Pulses & Pastas

To many, the thought of pulses, pasta and cereals is somewhat boring; all too frequently it evokes the unfavourable image wrongly associated with vegetarian diets: all lentils and beans.

In fact this is one of the most exciting chapters in *Lean Cuisine*, and the one that I most enjoyed creating. In the Mediterranean countries and the Middle East, dishes based on pulses and pasta have been part of the staple diet for centuries.

Pulses and pasta are not the fattening, stodgy foods that many people believe them to be. It is only an over-rich sauce or a generous quantity of oil that turns a rice or pasta dish into an unwise choice. They are all in fact naturally 'lean foods'.

Fresh pasta is now stocked by most of the major supermarkets, and specialist pasta shops are appearing in many towns. For those who are really keen, I have included a recipe for homemade pasta; it does take time but the quality of the result justifies the effort. Wholemeal pasta has the highest fibre content, but refined pasta is also a good source of protein.

There are many different types of rice available, so I have suggested the most suitable variety for each recipe. Brown rice dishes have the most wonderful 'nutty' texture and are also higher in fibre than those made with white rice.

All cereals, pulses and pasta require very careful cooking; if over-cooked, they become soggy and lose their natural texture. Brown rice and wholemeal pasta take a little longer to cook than refined varieties, but do test towards the end of the suggested cooking times. Always drain very thoroughly and, if necessary, return to a gentle heat to evaporate any excess moisture.

I think that these recipes will surprise and please you. Seafood and Soft Cheese Lasagne is one of my most popular recipes; so be prepared for your guests to come back for seconds! And couscous, with its unique texture, is one of the classic grain dishes and using the improvised method that I have suggested, you will find it very easy to cook.

SEAFOOD AND SOFT CHEESE LASAGNE

preparation: 20 minutes

cooking: 35—40 minutes

oven temperature: 190°C, 375°F, Gas Mark 5

serves 6

450 g/1 lb fresh spinach, cooked

freshly ground nutmeg

salt and freshly ground black pepper

3 tablespoons fromage blanc (page 140)

1 garlic clove, peeled and crushed

100 g/4 oz cooked, peeled prawns

100 g/4 oz shelled cooked mussels

1 egg yolk

225 g/8 oz dried green lasagne

100 g/4 oz low-fat soft cheese

150 ml/¼ pint homemade yogurt (page 139)

1 egg, beaten

2 tablespoons grated Parmesan cheese

to garnish:

sprigs of tarragon

1 Mix the drained and chopped spinach with the nutmeg, salt and pepper to taste; stir in the fromage blanc, garlic, peeled prawns, mussels and egg yolk.
2 Place half the spinach mixture in a lightly greased deep ovenproof dish; top with half the lasagne; add the soft cheese in small knobs, top with the remaining spinach mixture and then the rest of the lasagne.
3 To make the sauce, mix the yogurt with the egg and spoon over the top layer of lasagne. Sprinkle with the grated Parmesan cheese.
4 Bake in the preheated oven for 35—40 minutes, until bubbling and golden.
5 Serve piping hot in wedges garnished with tarragon and accompanied by a mixed salad.

Cook's Tip Choose a variety of lasagne that requires no pre-cooking.
Variation Instead of using shellfish, mix the spinach and fromage blanc mixture with chopped smoked chicken but still use the soft cheese.

For a special occasion, use a few smoked oysters, some chopped smoked salmon or some flaked crabmeat in the filling.

RICE WITH CORIANDER AND CASHEW NUTS

preparation: about 10 minutes

cooking: about 25 minutes

serves 4

225 g/8 oz long-grain brown rice

750 ml/1¼ pints chicken stock (page 139)

1 teaspoon saffron strands, soaked in

2 tablespoons boiling water

salt and freshly ground black pepper

2 tablespoons chopped coriander

2 garlic cloves, peeled and crushed

75 g/3 oz cashew nuts, chopped

to garnish (optional):

sprigs of fresh coriander

1 Put the rice, stock and strained saffron liquid into a pan; cover and bring to the boil. Stir once and simmer gently for about 25 minutes, until the rice is just tender.
2 Add salt and pepper to taste, the coriander, garlic and cashew nuts; cook, uncovered, for a further minute. All the liquid should have been absorbed.
3 Turn the cooked rice into a lightly oiled ring mould; allow to stand for 1 minute and then turn out carefully on a warm serving plate.
4 Serve immediately, filling the centre of the rice mould with sprigs of fresh coriander, if liked.

Cook's Tip Make sure that the rice has absorbed all the stock before you remove it from the heat; if necessary cook for a few minutes longer.
Variation Try using wild rice; it is more expensive but has a delicious nutty flavour.

Seafood and Soft Cheese Lasagne: *A mixture of spinach, low-fat cheese and shellfish makes an unusual creamy filling to layer with lasagne verdi and cook beneath a bubbling golden crust.*

GREEN RISOTTO

preparation: 5—10 minutes

cooking: about 35 minutes

serves 4—6

2 tablespoons olive oil

1 small onion, peeled and finely chopped

1 large garlic clove, peeled and chopped

450 g/1 lb Arborio (short-grain Italian) rice

1.6 litres/2¾ pints chicken stock (page 137)

450 g/1 lb spinach, cooked, drained and chopped

finely grated rind of ½ lemon

salt and freshly ground black pepper

2 tablespoons toasted pine kernels

1 Heat the oil and fry the onion and garlic gently for 3 minutes; add the rice and cook over a gentle heat for 5 minutes, stirring continuously. Do not allow the rice to colour.

2 Add 200 ml/⅓ pint of the chicken stock and simmer steadily until the stock has been absorbed. Add a further 200 ml/⅓ pint of the stock and the chopped spinach, and simmer again until the stock has been absorbed. Continue adding the stock gradually until it has been absorbed completely and the rice is tender.

3 Stir in the lemon rind, salt and pepper to taste and the pine kernels.

Cook's Tip Do use a good quality short-grain rice; a long-grain rice will not give such successful results.

Variation A short-grain brown rice can be used if preferred; the cooking time will be a little longer.

COUSCOUS WITH HOT PEPPERS

preparation: about 30 minutes

cooking: about 1 hour

serves 4

225 g/8 oz couscous

150 ml/¼ pint cold water

900 ml/1½ pints vegetable stock (page 137)

2 celery sticks, chopped

2 large carrots, peeled and sliced

1 medium onion, peeled and thinly sliced

small bunch of herbs (one variety, or mixed)

2 garlic cloves, peeled and crushed

2 tablespoons raisins

2 tablespoons chopped almonds

1 tablespoon chopped coriander

4 tomatoes, skinned, seeded and chopped

salt and freshly ground black pepper

1 tablespoon chilli sauce

1 Put the couscous into a large mixing bowl; sprinkle half the cold water over evenly, and work into the couscous with your fingertips.

2 Put the stock, vegetables, herbs and garlic into the base of the couscousier (see Cook's Tip) and bring to the boil; put the moistened couscous into the top of the couscousier, and place over the simmering stock.

3 Cover and steam over the simmering stock for 30 minutes; stir the grains with your fingers once or twice during this time.

4 Turn the couscous into a large bowl. Sprinkle with the remaining water and mix in evenly with your fingers or a wooden spoon, to separate the grains.

5 Mix in the raisins, almonds, coriander, tomatoes, and salt and pepper to taste, and return the couscous to the top of the couscousier.

6 Cover and steam for a further 30 minutes.

7 Stir the chilli sauce into the stock in the base of the pan and heat through.

8 Pile the hot couscous onto a warm serving dish and spoon the hot sauce and vegetables over the top. Serve immediately.

Cook's Tip A couscousier is a type of double saucepan; the bottom pan usually contains the sauce and/or meat, and the top perforated pan contains the couscous grain. If you do not have such a pan, use a saucepan with a large sieve that will fit neatly over the top.

Variation This recipe gets its title from the chilli sauce that is added at the end of cooking, and not from actual peppers. If you like a very pungent flavour, 1—2 finely sliced fresh chillies can be added to the vegetable and stock mixture.

BURGHUL WITH MINT AND EGG MIMOSA

preparation: 20 minutes, plus standing

serves 4

175 g/6 oz burghul (also known as bulghur)

3 spring onions, topped, tailed and finely chopped

2 tablespoons chopped mint

2 garlic cloves, peeled and crushed

salt and freshly ground black pepper

3 tablespoons olive oil

1½ tablespoons white wine vinegar

2 hard-boiled eggs

1 Soak the burghul in water for about 30 minutes, until it swells.

2 Drain the burghul, pressing out as much excess moisture as possible.

3 Mix the drained burghul with the spring onions, mint, garlic, and salt and pepper to taste. Mix the olive oil with the vinegar and stir into the burghul.

4 Separate the yolks and whites from the eggs; sieve the yolks and chop the whites finely.

5 Stir the egg whites into the burghul and spoon into a serving dish; sprinkle with the egg yolks.

Cook's Tip Burghul absorbs a lot of water so do make sure that you add sufficient water to cover the burghul generously.

Variation Add chopped toasted nuts in place of the hard-boiled eggs.

DHAL

preparation: about 10 minutes

cooking: 55 minutes

serves 4

225 g/8 oz green lentils, soaked in cold water overnight

1 medium onion, peeled and finely chopped

1 piece of fresh root ginger, bruised

2 bay leaves, crushed

2 fresh green chillies, chopped

1 tablespoon chopped coriander

3 tablespoons olive oil

2 large garlic cloves, peeled and crushed

1 teaspoon ground coriander

½ teaspoon ground cumin

½ teaspoon garam masala

salt

350 g/12 oz tomatoes, skinned, seeded and chopped

1 Drain the lentils and put them into a pan with the onion, root ginger, bay leaves, chillies, coriander, 1 tablespoon of the oil, and sufficient water to cover meanly; bring to the boil and simmer for about 45 minutes until the lentils are just tender. If the lentils become too dry, add a little extra liquid.

2 Heat the remaining oil and fry the garlic for 4−5 minutes. Add the ground coriander, cumin, and garam masala and fry for a further minute. Add salt to taste and the tomatoes, and heat through.

3 Stir the tomato and spice mixture into the lentils. Heat through gently for about 5 minutes.

4 Serve piping hot.

Cook's Tip If you have a pressure cooker, use it to cook the lentils; they will only take 5 minutes.

Variation The addition of 75 g/3 oz cooked spinach gives the most wonderful texture to the dhal.

PASTA SHELLS WITH AVOCADO AND SMOKED SALMON

preparation: 20 minutes

cooking: 8 minutes

serves 4

350 g/12 oz large pasta shells

2 tablespoons Basil and Garlic Oil (page 138)

dressing:

4 tablespoons mayonnaise

grated rind and juice of ½ lemon

4 tablespoons homemade yogurt (page 139)

2 tablespoons dry white wine

1 garlic clove, peeled and crushed

salt and freshly ground black pepper

1 tablespoon chopped chives

1 tablespoon orange lumpfish roe

100 g/4 oz smoked salmon, chopped

1 avocado, halved, stoned, peeled and chopped

to garnish:

small sprigs of basil

1 To make the dressing, mix the mayonnaise with the lemon rind and juice, yogurt, white wine, garlic, salt and pepper to taste, chives and lumpfish roe; stir in the salmon and avocado.

2 Cook the pasta shells in a large pan of boiling salted water for 8 minutes, or until just tender; drain thoroughly and toss in the Basil and Garlic Oil.

3 Toss the cooked pasta in the prepared sauce and serve immediately, garnished with sprigs of fresh basil.

Cook's Tip If you are using small pasta shells, reduce the cooking time slightly; do not stir the pasta while it is cooking, and make sure that the water is kept at a 'rolling boil'.

Variation For those who do not like avocado, substitute lightly scrambled egg or chopped hard-boiled egg. You can use wholewheat pasta shells, but they do take longer to cook.

SPAGHETTI WITH CHICKEN LIVERS AND LEMON

preparation: about 10 minutes

cooking: about 15 minutes

serves 4

350 g/12 oz wholemeal spaghetti

salt and freshly ground black pepper

1 small onion, peeled and finely chopped

2 tablespoons olive oil

225 g/8 oz chicken livers, chopped

finely grated rind of 1 lemon

1 garlic clove, peeled and crushed

4 tablespoons dry sherry

1 Lower the spaghetti into a large pan of steadily boiling water, to which you have added ½ teaspoon salt; cook for about 10 minutes until just tender.

2 Fry the onion in the olive oil for 3 minutes; add the chicken livers and lemon rind and continue frying until the livers are sealed on all sides. Season with salt and pepper.

3 Add the garlic and sherry, and allow to boil briskly for 1 minute.

4 Drain the spaghetti thoroughly and spoon onto a warm serving dish; spoon the prepared sauce over the top, and serve immediately.

Cook's Tip Do not overcook the chicken livers; like calves' liver, they should still be pink in the centre.

Variation Leftover red wine can be used instead of dry sherry if preferred.

Pasta Shells with Avocado and Smoked Salmon: *Pasta shells,
avocado and strips of smoked salmon catch the lumpfish roe and chive sauce as
it is spooned over this delicate mixture of ingredients.*

SPINACH GNOCCHI

preparation: about 30 minutes, plus chilling
cooking: 15–20 minutes
oven temperature: 190°C, 375°F, Gas Mark 5
serves 4

450 g/1 lb fresh spinach, cooked and drained

generous pinch of ground nutmeg

salt and freshly ground black pepper

75 g/3 oz wholemeal flour

150 g/5 oz curd cheese

2 egg yolks

3 tablespoons grated Parmesan cheese

40 g/1½ oz butter, melted

1 garlic clove, peeled and crushed

1 tablespoon chopped marjoram

1 Put the spinach into a liquidizer or food processor with the nutmeg, salt and pepper to taste, wholemeal flour, curd cheese, egg yolks and 1 tablespoon of the Parmesan cheese; blend to a soft dough.
2 Chill the gnocchi dough in a covered bowl for 3–4 hours.
3 Roll the dough out on a lightly floured surface to a thickness of just under 1 cm/½ inch. Using a plain pastry cutter, cut into circles about 4 cm/1½ inch in diameter.
4 Place the circles of gnocchi overlapping in a greased ovenproof dish; mix the melted butter with the garlic and marjoram and spoon over the gnocchi. Sprinkle with the remaining Parmesan.
5 Bake in the preheated oven for 15–20 minutes.

Cook's Tip Allow time to chill the dough very thoroughly; otherwise you will find it impossible to shape and cut.
Variation Instead of curd cheese you can use equal quantities of Ricotta and grated Cheddar.

CANNELLONI WITH RICOTTA

preparation: 25–30 minutes
cooking: about 40 minutes
oven temperature: 190°C, 375°F, Gas Mark 5
serves 4

100 g/4 oz button mushrooms, chopped

1 garlic clove, peeled and crushed

15 g/½ oz butter

3 tablespoons cooked peas

1 tablespoon chopped basil

1 bunch watercress, washed, drained and chopped

225 g/8 oz curd cheese

salt and freshly ground black pepper

8 cannelloni tubes

3 tablespoons homemade yogurt (page 139)

1 tablespoon chicken stock (page 137)

50 g/2 oz Edam or Gouda cheese, grated

1 Fry the mushrooms and garlic gently in the butter for about 3–4 minutes; mix in the peas, basil, watercress, curd cheese, and salt and pepper to taste.
2 Cook the cannelloni tubes in a large pan of boiling salted water; refresh under cold water and drain thoroughly but carefully.
3 Stuff each cannelloni tube with the curd cheese and vegetable filling, and place in a lightly greased ovenproof dish.
4 Mix the yogurt with the stock and spoon evenly over the cannelloni; sprinkle with the grated cheese.
5 Bake in the preheated oven for about 30 minutes until golden. Serve piping hot.

Cook's Tip If you do not have cannelloni tubes, you can use sheet lasagne; soften the sheets in boiling water and then roll around the prepared filling.
Variation Use 175 g/6 oz finely chopped or minced cooked chicken instead of the curd cheese.

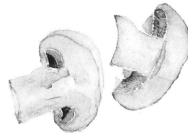

BROWN RICE KEDGEREE

preparation: 10 minutes

cooking: about 12 minutes

serves 4

•

1 small onion, peeled and finely chopped

1 garlic clove, peeled and crushed

1 tablespoon olive oil

3 tablespoons fromage blanc (page 140)

2 tablespoons chopped parsley

grated rind of ½ lemon

350 g/12 oz cooked brown rice

salt and freshly ground black pepper

225 g/8 oz cooked smoked haddock, flaked

2 hard-boiled eggs, roughly chopped

to garnish:

sprigs of parsley

1 Fry the onion and garlic gently in the oil for 4–5 minutes; do not allow to brown.

2 Stir in the fromage blanc, parsley and lemon rind, and heat through gently.

3 Add the rice, salt and pepper to taste, haddock and hard-boiled eggs, and stir over a gentle heat for a few minutes.

4 Serve piping hot on a warm serving dish garnished with parsley sprigs.

Cook's Tip Make sure that the cooked rice is well drained before it is incorporated into the kedgeree; a kedgeree should be moist, but not sloppy.

Variation All sorts of smoked fish can be used very successfully in a kedgeree, for example, smoked mackerel or smoked salmon trimmings.

HOMEMADE FETTUCCINE

preparation: about 50 minutes, plus standing

cooking: 2–3 minutes

serves 4–6

•

450 g/1 lb strong plain flour

1 teaspoon salt

3–4 eggs, beaten

1 tablespoon olive oil

extra flour for rolling

1 Sieve the flour and salt either into a mound on a clean work surface, or into a large mixing bowl; make a well in the centre and add the eggs and olive oil.

2 Work to a smooth dough. Knead the dough on a lightly floured work surface until it is smooth and elastic. This is very similar to making bread dough.

3 Wrap the dough in a damp cloth and leave to stand at room temperature for 30 minutes.

4 Divide the dough in half. Roll each piece of dough out in turn on a lightly floured work surface, until it is paper-thin and you can almost see through it.

5 Roll each sheet up quite loosely, as for a Swiss roll, and cut through at 5 mm/¼ inch intervals. Unroll the thin strips of dough carefully.

6 Lower into a pan of steadily boiling salted water and cook for just 2–3 minutes.

7 Drain thoroughly and serve as an accompaniment to main course dishes, or tossed in a little butter and served with grated Parmesan cheese as a separate pasta dish.

Cook's Tip If you have a pasta machine, this will save a great deal of time both in shaping and cutting the fettuccine. To store the fettuccine, hang the strips over a lightly floured teatowel, over the back of a chair, for about 1 hour; then pack in waxed paper or cling film and store in the refrigerator or freezer.

Variation Use wholemeal flour instead of plain white flour and add a little extra beaten egg if necessary. For green fettuccine, add 100 g/4 oz cooked, drained and chopped spinach with the eggs and olive oil.

FETTUCCINE WITH WALNUT AND CHEESE SAUCE

preparation: 10–15 minutes

cooking: 13–15 minutes

serves 4

1 medium onion, peeled and finely chopped

2 tablespoons olive oil

1 garlic clove, peeled and chopped

1 tablespoon chopped thyme

150 ml/¼ pint dry white wine

2 egg yolks

3 tablespoons homemade yogurt (page 139), or crème fraîche

salt and freshly ground black pepper

75 g/3 oz walnuts, chopped,

4 tablespoons grated Parmesan cheese

350 g/12 oz green fettuccine (page 103)

to garnish:

chopped coriander

1 Fry the onion gently in the olive oil with the garlic for 3–4 minutes; add the thyme and fry for a further minute.

2 Add the white wine and simmer for 2–3 minutes; beat the egg yolks with the yogurt or crème fraîche and stir into the wine mixture. Stir over a gentle heat for 1 minute, adding salt and pepper to taste. Add the walnuts and the Parmesan cheese.

3 Meanwhile cook the fettuccine in boiling salted water for just 3 minutes; drain thoroughly.

4 Toss the cooked pasta in the prepared sauce. Sprinkle with coriander and serve immediately.

Cook's Tip If you want to keep the sauce warm, put it into a double saucepan or a basin over a pan of hot water.

Variation Try serving a mixture of pasta, half green and half yellow fettuccine, for example.

WHOLEMEAL SPAGHETTI CARBONARA

preparation: about 10 minutes

cooking: about 15 minutes

serves 4

2 tablespoons olive oil

1 small onion, peeled and finely chopped

350 g/12 oz wholemeal spaghetti

salt and freshly ground black pepper

4 slices lean ham, chopped

4 tablespoons dry white wine

3 eggs

50 g/2 oz Parmesan cheese, grated

1 tablespoon chopped parsley

1 tablespoon chopped basil

2 garlic cloves, peeled and crushed

1 Heat the oil and fry the onion for 3–4 minutes.

2 Lower the spaghetti into a large pan of steadily boiling water, to which you have added ½ teaspoon salt; cook for about 10 minutes until just tender.

3 Meanwhile add the chopped ham to the onion and fry for 1 minute; add the wine and cook until the wine has almost completely evaporated.

4 Beat the eggs with the cheese, parsley, basil, garlic, and salt and pepper to taste.

5 Drain the spaghetti thoroughly and keep warm.

6 Stir in the egg and ham mixtures; the residual heat from the spaghetti will be sufficient to cook the egg lightly.

7 Spoon onto a hot serving dish and serve immediately.

Cook's Tip Although wholemeal pasta takes slightly longer to cook than the standard variety, it is important to check the texture carefully; if it is overcooked, it is spoilt.

Variation Try using a smoked ham, such as Parma, in place of ordinary ham.

Fettucine with Walnut and Cheese Sauce: *A forkful of flavour-thin ribbons of green pasta are topped with a white wine, walnut and Parmesan sauce.*

Desserts

The dessert can be the crowning glory of a meal; indeed, few can resist the tempting puddings that complete a special occasion. I have even heard friends say that they would rather miss the main course and have two puddings! But sticky confections of chocolate, layers of creamy meringue and calorie-laden gateaux have no place in *Lean Cuisine*.

Lean Cuisine is still going to tempt you, but with a very special 'dessert trolley'. All the desserts in this chapter are agreeably sweet, but they are sweetened subtly, sometimes with muscovado sugar, sometimes with honey and sometimes with a little liqueur. It is worth remembering that many of the flavours that we associate with luscious desserts owe very little to the actual sugar content and far more to the fresh fruits, grated fruit rinds, spices, nuts etc. which are so frequently used.

Mousses get their creamy texture from homemade yogurt; jellies are made from freshly prepared fruit juices; custards are made from low-calorie skimmed milk, as in Passion Fruit and Lemon Custard; and the delicious Cherry Ice Cream uses homemade yogurt rather than cream. Your family and friends will be greatly impressed by any of these lean desserts, and will be enchanted by their light textures and fresh flavours.

There are also *Lean Cuisine* versions of such firm favourites as syllabubs, fruit fools and pancakes. After tasting these, you will not want to revert to using lavish amounts of cream and sugar.

Most of the desserts can be made in advance so that they can be enjoyed the following day or the day after. Some of the puddings such as the Kiwi Fruit Sorbet and the Pineapple Granita can be made and kept in the freezer so that you have a tempting selection of ready prepared desserts 'on ice'. This will prove invaluable when you are entertaining or very pushed for time.

All the desserts look as good as they taste. Offer your *Lean Cuisine* 'dessert trolley' with pride; even those with a sweet tooth will leave your table satisfied.

FIGS IN SHERRIED YOGURT

preparation: 15—20 minutes

serves 4

12 fresh figs

3 tablespoons chopped shelled pistachios

6 dried aprictos, finely chopped

pinch of mixed spice

1 teaspoon grated orange rind

6 tablespoons homemade yogurt (page 139)

1 tablespoon medium-dry sherry

to decorate:

split pistachios

thin strips of orange peel

1 Make a criss-cross cut in the top of each fresh fig, and open each one out slightly.
2 Mix the pistachios, apricots, spice and orange rind together; press some of this mixture gently into the centre of each fig.
3 Mix the yogurt with the sherry and put a spoonful onto four dessert plates; carefully arrange three stuffed figs on each plate.
4 Scatter the split pistachios over the top and arrange the strips of orange peel at the edge of each plate.

Cook's Tip Choose figs that are ripe yet firm enough to cut into a good shape; over-ripe figs will collapse as soon as pressure is put on them. Chilling in the refrigerator for 1—2 hours will make them a little firmer.
Variation Stuff the figs with a little softened leftover marzipan; but use a variety that does not contain too much sugar. Flavour the yogurt with a little almond- or apricot-flavoured liqueur rather than sherry.

LIME AND MANGO PARFAIT

preparation: 25 minutes, plus chilling

serves 4—6

450 ml/¾ pint fresh mango purée

finely grated rind of 2 limes

juice of 1 lime

25 g/1 oz soft brown sugar

4 tablespoons quark

15 g/½ oz powdered gelatine

3 tablespoons water

2 egg whites

to decorate:

twists of lime peel

1 Mix the mango purée with the lime rind and juice, brown sugar and quark.
2 Put the gelatine and water into a small bowl and set aside for 1 minute; stand the bowl in a pan of hot water and leave until the gelatine has dissolved, about 2 minutes.
3 Stir the gelatine into the mango mixture and leave on one side until it starts to thicken.
4 Whisk the egg whites until stiff but not dry; fold lightly but thoroughly into the semi-set mango mixture.
5 Spoon into tall stemmed glasses and decorate with twists of lime peel. Chill for 1 hour.

Cook's Tip It is better to keep the limes at room temperature than to chill them, as this makes it easier to grate the rind and squeeze the juice.
Variation Orange also blends well with mango. Use orange rind and juice instead of lime, and decorate with twists of orange peel.

Figs in Sherried Yogurt: *Petals of fresh figs enclose a sweet stuffing of
dried apricots, orange rind and pistachio nuts.*

CHERRY ICE CREAM

preparation: 20 minutes, plus freezing

serves 4

•

3 eggs, separated

1 tablespoon golden granulated sugar

200 ml/⅓ pint homemade yogurt (page 139)

150 g/5 oz fresh sweet cherries, stoned
and halved

1 Whisk the egg yolks and sugar until thick and creamy; mix in the yogurt.
2 Whisk the egg whites until stiff but not dry; fold lightly but thoroughly into the egg yolk mixture, together with the cherries.
3 Pour into a shallow container, about 5 cm/2 inch deep; freeze until solid enough to scoop – about 4–6 hours.
4 Leave at room temperature for a few minutes before scooping into serving glasses.

Cook's Tip This ice cream is called a one-stage ice cream; it does not need beating during freezing.
Variation A little liqueur can be added to the basic ice cream mixture; Kirsch is particularly good with cherries.

TROPICAL-STYLE FRUIT SALAD

preparation: 15 minutes, plus standing and chilling

serves 4

•

100 g/4 oz desiccated coconut

300 ml/½ pint boiling water

25 g/1 oz soft brown sugar

grated rind of 1 lime

3 tablespoons white rum

2 slices fresh pineapple, peeled and cut
into chunks

3 kiwi fruit, peeled and sliced

1 small mango, halved, stoned, peeled and
sliced

½ small melon, seeded and scooped
into small balls

1 small ripe pawpaw, peeled, halved,
seeded and sliced

1 Put the desiccated coconut into a bowl and pour on the boiling water; leave to stand for 30 minutes.
2 Press the coconut milk through a sieve into a decorative glass bowl. Add the lime rind and rum.
3 Add the prepared fruits, mixing them well with the coconut liquid.
4 Cover and chill for 2–3 hours.

Cook's Tip Do not overchill the salad, as this would make the fruits lose their characteristic colours.
Variation Instead of coconut milk, any unsweetened fruit juice, such as pineapple or apple, can be used as a base.

REAL LEMON MOUSSE

preparation: 25 minutes, plus chilling

serves 4

3 eggs, separated

75 g/3 oz soft brown sugar

grated rind and juice of 2 lemons

15 g/½ oz powdered gelatine

3 tablespoons cold water

to decorate:

twists of lemon peel

1 Put the yolks and soft brown sugar into a bowl; whisk until thick, light and creamy.
2 Mix in the lemon rind and juice.
3 Put the gelatine and water into a small bowl and set aside for 1 minute; stand the bowl in a pan of hot water and leave until the gelatine has dissolved, about 2 minutes.
4 Stir the dissolved gelatine into the egg mixture; leave to cool until the mixture is on the point of setting.
5 Whisk the egg whites until stiff but not dry, and fold lightly but thoroughly into the lemon mixture.
6 Spoon into tall sundae glasses and chill until set.
7 Decorate with lemon peel twists.

Cook's Tip If you like a strong citrus flavour, use only 50 g/2 oz of sugar.
Variation For a lime mousse, substitute 3 limes for the 2 lemons.

CHEESE MOUSSE WITH REDCURRANTS

preparation: 25 minutes, plus chilling

serves 6

350 g/12 oz curd cheese

50 g/2 oz soft brown sugar

300 ml/½ pint homemade yogurt
(page 139)

275 g/10 oz fresh redcurrants, topped and tailed

15 g/½ oz powdered gelatine

3 tablespoons water

2 tablespoons Crème de Cassis

to decorate:

75 g/3 oz redcurrants, lightly cooked in a little orange juice

small mint leaves

1 Put the curd cheese into a liquidizer or food processor with the sugar, yogurt, 175 g/6 oz of the redcurrants; blend until smooth.
2 Put the gelatine and water into a small bowl and set aside for 1 minute; stand in a pan of hot water and leave until dissolved, about 2 minutes. Stir the gelatine and Cassis into the redcurrant and cheese mixture and leave in a cool place for about 15 minutes.
3 Fold in the remaining redcurrants; spoon into a 5 cm/2 inch deep serving dish and chill briefly until set.
4 To serve, scoop out the mousse with a dampened dessert spoon, placing three scoops on each plate.
5 Spoon over the cooked redcurrants with a little of the orange juice and decorate with mint leaves.

Cook's Tip To top and tail the redcurrants, pull each sprig gently through the prongs of a fork.
Variation Blackcurrants make a perfect alternative to redcurrants.

MARINATED PEACHES

preparation: 15 minutes, plus chilling

serves 4

4 large ripe fresh peaches

4 teaspoons Crème de Cassis

200 ml/⅓ pint sparkling dry white wine, chilled

to decorate:

4 bay leaves

1 Make a nick in the stalk end of each peach; plunge into a bowl of boiling water for 45 seconds. Lift out and peel off the skins.
2 Place each peach in a small glass serving dish; spoon over the liqueur and add the sparkling white wine.
3 Chill for 30 minutes.
4 Decorate each peach with a small bay leaf.

Cook's Tip If the peaches are very ripe, blanch them for a slightly shorter time. Before blanching, test the skins at the stalk end; if they come away easily, peel with a knife as there is less chance of discoloration if you can avoid blanching the fruit.
Variation Fresh apricots can be treated in a similar manner; allow 2 large apricots per person.

STRAWBERRY TERRINE

preparation: 30 minutes, plus chilling

serves 6

300 ml/½ pint fresh orange juice

300 ml/½ pint water

2 tablespoons Grand Marnier

5 teaspoons powdered gelatine

handful of large mint leaves

450 g/1 lb fresh strawberries, hulled and sliced

to decorate:

6 whole strawberries, hulled, sliced and fanned

thin strips of orange peel (optional)

small sprigs of mint or basil

1 Lightly oil a 1 kg/2 lb loaf tin or terrine.
2 Put the gelatine and 3 tablespoons of the water into a small bowl and set aside for 1 minute. Stand the bowl in a pan of hot water and leave until the gelatine has dissolved, about 2 minutes.
3 Mix the orange juice with the remaining water, and the Grand Marnier.
4 Add the dissolved gelatine to the fruit juice mixture, stirring until well blended. Chill in the freezer briefly until the mixture starts to turn syrupy.
5 Spoon a little of the syrupy jelly over the base and sides of the loaf tin or terrine and line with mint leaves; chill in the freezer briefly.
6 Mix the remaining jelly with the sliced strawberries; spoon into the prepared tin or terrine. Chill in the refrigerator until firm enough to cut.
7 Carefully unmould the set terrine and cut into slices; place each one on a dessert plate and decorate with fanned-out strawberries, strips of orange peel, if liked, and mint or basil sprigs.

Cook's Tip If the set terrine is at all temperamental, it may need dipping briefly into hot water to loosen it, prior to unmoulding.
Variation Any other fruit which holds its shape fairly well can be used in such a terrine recipe – for example, peeled orange segments, sliced kiwi fruit or sliced peaches.

Jellied Strawberry Terrine: *Slivers of strawberry are set in orange and
Grand Marnier jelly to form a pretty terrine. Serve it in thin slices with fans of
fresh strawberries.*

PINEAPPLE GRANITA

preparation: about 10 minutes, plus freezing

cooking: about 5 minutes

serves 4

75 g/3 oz golden granulated sugar

300 ml/½ pint water

peeled rind of ½ orange

juice of 1 orange

3 slices peeled fresh pineapple, chopped

to decorate:

bay leaves

small wedges of fresh pineapple

1 Put the sugar, water and orange peel into a pan; stir over a gentle heat until the sugar has dissolved. Simmer for 4–5 minutes.

2 Strain the syrup into a liquidizer or food processor and add the orange juice and chopped pineapple; blend until puréed. The mixture will still be textured. Allow to cool.

3 Pour into a shallow container and freeze without stirring for 2 hours, until the granita has the texture of slushy snow.

4 Spoon into tall glasses and decorate each portion with a bay leaf and a small wedge of pineapple.

Cook's Tip The granita can be frozen for much longer than the suggested 2 hours. In this case leave the frozen granita at room temperature, stirring it from time to time, until it is of the right consistency to serve.

Variation If you do not want to buy a pineapple specially for this dessert, use pineapple canned in natural juice and well drained.

KIWI FRUIT SORBET

preparation: 20 minutes, plus freezing

cooking: 3 minutes

serves 4

5 kiwi fruit, peeled and roughly chopped

75 g/3 oz soft bown sugar

150 ml/¼ pint water

juice of 1 lemon

2 egg whites

1 Place the kiwi fruit in a liquidizer or food processor; blend until smooth.

2 Put the sugar and water into a pan; stir over a gentle heat until dissolved. Bring to the boil and simmer for 3 minutes.

3 Stir the kiwi fruit purée into the sugar syrup with the lemon juice and leave to cool.

4 Pour into a shallow container and freeze until slushy; beat in a bowl to break up the ice crystals.

5 Whisk the egg whites until stiff but not dry; fold lightly but thoroughly into the semi-set sorbet.

6 Return to the container and freeze until just firm.

7 Scoop the sorbet into stemmed glasses and serve immediately.

Cook's Tip Some people do not like the pips in kiwi fruit; you can sieve the purée if preferred.

Variation Try using fresh figs when they are in season.

SPICED RHUBARB FOOL

preparation: 10 minutes, plus chilling

cooking: about 10 minutes

serves 4

450 g/1 lb young rhubarb, cut into short lengths

2 tablespoons orange juice

small piece of fresh root ginger, crushed

50 g/2 oz soft brown sugar

300 ml/½ pint homemade yogurt (page 139)

to decorate:

twists of orange peel

1 Put the rhubarb into a pan with the orange juice and ginger; cover and cook gently for about 10 minutes until the rhubarb is just tender. Sieve into a bowl and leave to cool.

2 Add the sugar and chill thoroughly.

3 Mix in the yogurt, just swirling it, rather than mixing it in completely, to give a marbled effect.

4 Spoon into tall glasses and decorate with orange peel twists.

Cook's Tip Fresh rhubarb does not have a very strong pink colour; add a few drops of pink colouring to enhance this.

Variation Fold in some chopped peeled orange segments with the yogurt.

PRUNE SYLLABUB

preparation: 15 minutes, plus chilling and soaking

cooking: 5 minutes

serves 4

175 g/6 oz prunes, stoned

300 ml/½ pint dry white wine

150 ml/¼ pint homemade yogurt (page 139)

1 tablespoon brandy

to decorate:

twists of orange peel

1 Soak the prunes in the white wine overnight, until well plumped.

2 Put the prunes and their liquid into a pan and simmer for 5 minutes.

3 Place the prunes and their liquid in a liquidizer or food processor; blend until smooth. Allow to cool.

4 Mix the prune purée with the yogurt and brandy and spoon into tall stemmed glasses; chill briefly.

5 Decorate each one with an orange peel twist.

Cook's Tip If the prunes are really well plumped after soaking, there is no need to simmer them for 5 minutes; bite into one to test it.

Variation Other dried fruits such as figs or apricots can be used.

FRUIT PICTURES

preparation: 20 minutes

serves 4

300 ml/½ pint homemade yogurt (page 139)

2 tablespoons Cointreau

2 tablespoons fresh raspberry purée, sieved

2 passion fruit, halved

2 kiwi fruit, peeled and thinly sliced

4 whole strawberries, hulled, sliced and fanned

2 fresh figs, sliced

10 black grapes, halved

2 nectarines, halved, stoned and sliced

1 large orange, peeled and segmented

12 fresh raspberries or blackcurrants

to decorate:

fresh mint leaves

1 Mix the yogurt with the Cointreau and spoon onto four dessert plates.
2 Put a small spoonful of the raspberry purée into the centre of the yogurt on each plate; using the tip of a small knife drag the purée through the yogurt. Spoon a little of the passion fruit pulp into the centre of each plate.
3 Arrange the prepared fruits decoratively in sections, around the purée.
4 Serve immediately, decorated with mint leaves.

Cook's Tip If you are planning to serve this dessert at a dinner party, have a practice run first and experiment on a plate.
Variation Other liqueurs can be used to flavour the yogurt; try using other fruits such as balls of melon, sections of mango, wedges of fresh fig and redcurrants.

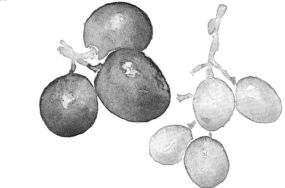

ORANGE SNOW EGGS

preparation: 25–30 minutes

cooking: about 30 minutes

oven temperature: 160°C, 325°F, Gas Mark 3

serves 4

3 eggs, separated

300 ml/½ pint homemade yogurt (page 139)

50 g/2 oz soft brown sugar

finely grated rind of 1 orange

about 300 ml/½ pint skimmed milk

peeled segments of 2 oranges

1 Beat the egg yolks with the yogurt, half the sugar and the orange rind; pour into a shallow ovenproof dish.
2 Stand the dish in a roasting tin and add hot water to come halfway up the sides. Bake in the preheated oven for about 20–25 minutes, until just set. Remove from the oven and allow to cool.
3 Heat the skimmed milk gently in a frying pan. Whisk the egg whites until stiff but not dry, and then whisk in the remaining brown sugar.
4 Slide spoonfuls of the meringue mixture into the simmering milk; poach gently for 3–4 minutes, turning the meringues once. Drain briefly on paper towels.
5 Arrange the orange segments on top of the cooled custard and then arrange the cooked meringues on the top.
6 Serve within 1 hour of finishing.

Cook's Tip Do not overcook the base custard, as this would make it too firm.
Variation Flavour the custard with orange rind as above but top it with slices of fresh peach instead of orange segments.

Fruit Pictures: *An artist's palate of colour, flavour and texture. This
assortment of prepared fruits and feathered raspberry purée creates
an edible picture.*

POACHED APPLES WITH MINT

preparation: 10 minutes, plus chilling

cooking: 12−15 minutes

serves 4

300 ml/½ pint pure apple juice

2 tablespoons golden granulated sugar

grated rind and juice of 1 lemon

2 tablespoons chopped mint

4 cloves

4 dessert apples, peeled, halved and cored

to decorate:

sprigs of mint

1 Put the apple juice, sugar, lemon rind and juice, and mint into a pan with the cloves; stir over a gentle heat until the sugar has dissolved.
2 Add the prepared apples to the syrup; cover the pan and poach gently for about 12−15 minutes, until the apples are just tender.
3 Allow the apples to cool in their syrup and then chill.
4 Spoon the apples into four small glass dishes; spoon over a little of the strained chilled syrup and decorate with sprigs of mint.

Cook's Tip While preparing the apples put them into a bowl of acidulated water (water with lemon juice added) to prevent them from discolouring.
Variation This recipe can also be made with peeled, halved and cored fresh pears.

NORMANDY PANCAKES

preparation: 20 minutes

cooking: about 16 minutes

serves 4

100 g/4 oz wholemeal flour

¼ teaspoon ground ginger

1 egg

300 ml/½ pint skimmed milk

grated rind of ½ lemon

filling:

300 ml/½ pint unsweetened apple purée

50 g/2 oz raisins

1 tablespoon brandy

to decorate:

2 tablespoons toasted flaked almonds

1 To make the filling, mix the apple purée with the raisins and brandy.
2 Put the wholemeal flour and ginger into a bowl; make a well in the centre and add the egg and half the skimmed milk. Beat until smooth and then gradually beat in the remaining skimmed milk and the lemon rind.
3 Using a small non-stick pan, make the batter into eight small pancakes, allowing about 1 minute for each side. Keep the pancakes warm by stacking them between sheets of non-stick silicone or greased greaseproof paper.
4 When all the pancakes are made, put a little of the apple filling in the centre of each pancake and roll up.
5 Sprinkle with the toasted nuts and serve immediately.

Cook's Tip The contrast between warm pancake and cold filling is very good; but you can warm the filling through, if preferred.
Variation Use other seasonal fruits like raspberries or strawberries as a filling for the pancakes.

POACHED PEARS WITH COFFEE SAUCE

preparation: 15 minutes

cooking: about 20 minutes

serves 4

4 under-ripe pears

½ lemon

300 ml/½ pint dry cider

1 tablespoon soft brown sugar

piece of cinnamon stick

3 egg yolks

150 ml/¼ pint fairly strong black coffee

2 tablespoons Tia Maria

1 Peel the pears, leaving the stalk intact if possible; remove the core from the base of each pear.
2 Rub the pears all over with the cut lemon; put into a pan and add the cider, sugar and cinnamon stick. Bring to the boil, cover, and poach gently until the pears are just tender; they will need turning from time to time.
3 Put the egg yolks, coffee and liqueur into a double saucepan, or into a bowl over a pan of hot water, and whisk until thick, light and fluffy.
4 Drain the warm pears from their poaching liquid; place on small individual plates and spoon over the warm coffee sauce. Serve immediately.

Cook's Tip Rub the pears well with the lemon as they discolour very quickly, especially if very under-ripe. The poaching liquid can be used again to cook other fruits.
Variation Instead of serving the poached pears with a coffee sauce, use one based on fresh redcurrants when they are in season.

BLACKBERRY JELLY

preparation: 20 minutes, plus chilling

cooking: 25 minutes

serves 4

350 g/12 oz fresh blackberries

600 ml/1 pint water

3 tablespoons golden granulated sugar

4 teaspoons powdered gelatine

3 tablespoons water

2 tablespoons port

to decorate:

fresh blackberries, preferably with leaves

1 Put the blackberries into a pan with the water and sugar; bring to the boil and simmer gently for 25 minutes.
2 Strain through a sieve into a bowl, pressing on the blackberries to extract as much juice as possible; measure off exactly 600 ml/1 pint blackberry juice.
3 Put the gelatine and the 3 tablespoons of water into a small bowl and set aside for 1 minute; stand the bowl in a pan of hot water and leave until the gelatine has dissolved, about 2 minutes.
4 Stir the dissolved gelatine into the measured blackberry juice; pour into a lightly oiled 600 ml/1 pint mould. Chill for 4 hours until set.
5 Carefully unmould the set jelly onto a serving plate. Decorate with some fresh blackberries and their leaves.

Cook's Tip Any surplus prepared blackberry juice can be chilled and poured over the unmoulded jelly when serving.
Variation Fresh redcurrants and blackcurrants also make a very good fresh fruit jelly; use the same quantities as above, adjusting the sugar slightly to taste.

PASSION FRUIT AND LEMON CUSTARD

preparation: 20 minutes, plus chilling

cooking: about 15 minutes

serves 4

50 g/2 oz golden granulated sugar

4 egg yolks

450 ml/¾ pint semi-skimmed milk

few drops of vanilla essence

finely grated rind of 1 lemon

15 g/½ oz powdered gelatine

3 tablespoons water

to decorate:

6 passion fruit

grated lemon rind

lemon peel 'leaves' (see Cook's Tip)

1 Put the sugar and egg yolks into a bowl; whisk until soft, light and creamy.
2 Heat the milk in a pan and whisk onto the egg yolk mixture; add the vanilla extract and the grated lemon rind. Put into the top of a double saucepan and stir over a gentle heat until the custard coats the back of a wooden spoon.
3 Mix the gelatine with the water in a small bowl and set aside for 1 minute. Stand the bowl in a pan of hot water and leave until the gelatine has dissolved, about 2 minutes. Add to the cooled custard.
4 Lightly oil a 600 ml/1 pint mould and pour in the custard mixture; chill for at least 4 hours until set.
5 Meanwhile halve the passion fruit and scoop out the pulp.
6 Carefully turn the set custard out onto a flat serving dish and spoon the passion fruit pulp decoratively around it. Decorate with lemon rind and lemon peel 'leaves'.

Cook's Tip Use a mould that has a well-defined shape, so that the custard looks attractive when turned out. If the weather is really warm when you make this pudding, add an extra teaspoon of powdered gelatine.
To make lemon peel 'leaves', thinly pare the rind from 1 lemon in wide strips and cut into leaf shapes using small scissors.
Variation Add 2 passion fruit, scooped out, to the cool custard mixture, before putting it into the mould to set. The custard can also be set in small individual moulds; this looks particularly pretty for a dinner party.

APRICOT AND ALMOND BRULEE

preparation: 15 minutes

cooking: about 35 minutes

oven temperature: 160°C, 325°F, Gas Mark 3

serves 4

350 g/12 oz fresh apricots, halved, stoned and skinned

300 ml/½ pint homemade yogurt (page 139)

3 eggs

2 tablespoons soft brown sugar

few drops of almond essence

3 tablespoons flaked almonds

1 Place the halved apricots in a lightly greased flameproof dish, about 600 ml/1 pint capacity.
2 Beat the yogurt with the eggs, 1 tablespoon of the sugar and the almond essence. Pour over the apricots.
3 Stand the dish in a roasting tin; add sufficient hot water to come halfway up the sides. Bake in the oven for 30–35 minutes, until just set.
4 Remove from the oven, sprinkle with the flaked almonds and remaining sugar to give an even coating, and place under a preheated grill for 2–3 minutes.
5 Serve immediately.

Cook's Tip This does not have the same sugary topping as a traditional 'brûlée'; it is less rich and much healthier.
Variation Apricots canned in natural juice can be substituted when the fresh ones are out of season.

Passion Fruit and Lemon Custard: *A light lemon custard is set in beautiful heart shapes, surrounded by fragrant passion fruit and finally topped with lemon peel leaves.*

121

Baking

There is no doubt that homebaked cakes and biscuits are superior to their shop-bought counterparts. Their texture is usually lighter and more moist, the flavour is fresher, and there is always the added satisfaction of enjoying something that has been specially baked. There is nothing quite so appetizing as the warm aroma that permeates the kitchen when a fruit cake or a batch of bread is in the oven – almost a reward in itself for your work.

Like desserts, cakes and biscuits are often considered by health-conscious eaters as 'forbidden foods'. It was therefore quite a challenge creating recipes that exemplify the tenets of *Lean Cuisine*. You will find that all of them are nutritious, not *too* sweet, relatively low in calories, and with that wonderful home-baked flavour. So what is the secret?

Wholemeal flour has been used wherever possible; mixtures have been enriched with yogurt or curd cheese to cut down on the fat; and certain surprise ingredients have been included: fresh plum purée in a teabread, grated carrot in muffins and chopped fresh pineapple in a cake. Much of the sweetness in these teatime delights comes from dried fruits — a far better way of sweetening than using lots of sugar.

To enjoy homemade cakes and biscuits at their best, they should be kept really fresh. Store biscuits and cookies in an airtight tin or plastic container, wrap cakes securely in cling film or foil, and store breads in a bread crock or bread bin.

Banana Muffins are delicious served warm at breakfast and are sufficiently moist to need no butter; the Wholemeal Bread Sticks make a really good accompaniment to soups; and Ginger Oatcakes are wonderful with a mid-morning cup of coffee. These are just some of the treats to come from the *Lean Cuisine* bakery.

PLUM, APRICOT AND PRUNE TEABREAD

preparation: 15 minutes

cooking: about 1½ hours

oven temperature: 170°C, 325°F, Gas Mark 3

makes 1 × 1 kg/2 lb loaf

●

225 g/8 oz wholemeal flour

50 g/2 oz ground almonds

2 teaspoons baking powder

3 eggs

150 ml/¼ pint thick homemade yogurt
(page 139)

150 ml/¼ pint plum purée, unsweetened
(made from stoned ripe plums)

75 g/3 oz soft dark brown sugar

75 g/3 oz dried apricots, coarsely chopped

75 g/3 oz stoned prunes, coarsely chopped

75 g/3 oz hazelnuts

topping:

2 tablespoons chopped hazelnuts

1 Grease and line a 1 kg/2 lb loaf tin with non-stick silicone or greased greaseproof paper.
2 Put the flour, ground almonds, baking powder, eggs, yogurt, plum purée and sugar into a large mixing bowl; beat for 2−3 minutes until thoroughly mixed.
3 Mix in the apricots, prunes and whole hazelnuts.
4 Transfer the mixture to the prepared tin, smoothing the surface level. Sprinkle with chopped nuts.
5 Bake in the preheated oven for about 1½ hours, until cooked right through; test with a fine skewer.
6 Allow the teabread to stand for a few minutes in its tin before turning onto a wire rack to cool.

Cook's Tip Because the teabread mixture is quite rich, it is important to line the tin very carefully to avoid the mixture catching or burning during baking.
Variation Other dried fruits can be used instead of the apricots and prunes; for example, chopped dried figs, dates or peaches.

YOGURT AND PECAN SCONES

preparation: 20 minutes

cooking: 15 minutes

oven temperature: 220°C, 425°F, Gas Mark 7

makes about 12

●

225 g/8 oz wholemeal flour

2 teaspoons baking powder

generous pinch of salt

40 g/1½ oz butter

1 tablespoon soft brown sugar

150 ml/¼ pint homemade yogurt (page 139)

3 tablespoons chopped pecan nuts

2 tablespoons skimmed milk

12 pecan halves

1 Sieve the flour, baking powder and salt into a bowl; rub in the butter.
2 Add the sugar, yogurt and pecan nuts and mix to a soft dough.
3 Roll out the dough on a lightly floured work surface to a depth of about 2 cm/¾ inch; cut into twelve rounds using a fluted pastry cutter.
4 Place the shaped scones on a lightly greased baking sheet; glaze with skimmed milk and press a half pecan into each scone.
5 Bake in the preheated oven for about 15 minutes, until risen and pale golden.
6 Serve warm.

Cook's Tip If you are making the scones in advance, allow them to cool and store in an airtight tin. Reheat the scones, wrapped in foil, in a moderately hot oven.
Variation Shelled peanuts make a good alternative to chopped pecans; sprinkle roughly chopped peanuts on the scones prior to baking.

Plum, Apricot and Prune Teabread *and* **Yogurt and Pecan
Scones:** *Nutty treats for teatime.*

BANANA MUFFINS

preparation: 10 minutes

cooking: 20 minutes

oven temperature: 190°C, 375°F, Gas Mark 5

makes about 10

2 ripe bananas, peeled

25 g/1 oz soft dark brown sugar

1 egg, beaten

100 g/4 oz raw carrots, finely grated

2 tablespoons homemade yogurt (page 139)

100 g/4 oz wholemeal flour

1½ teaspoons baking powder

generous pinch of ground ginger

2 tablespoons crushed dried banana flakes

1 Fit paper cake cases into ten small patty tins.
2 Mash the bananas with the sugar until smooth; beat in the egg, grated carrots and yogurt.
3 Put the flour, baking powder and ginger into a bowl; beat in the banana and carrot mixture with the banana flakes.
4 Divide the mixture between the paper cases.
5 Bake in the preheated oven for about 20 minutes, until risen and just firm to the touch.
6 Allow to cool slightly and serve warm.

Cook's Tip The best method of preparing the carrot is to use the shredder blade of a food processor; a cheese grater does not give such a good texture.
Variation Unpeeled grated apple can be used instead of grated carrot.

WHOLEMEAL BREAD STICKS

preparation: 30 minutes, plus proving

cooking: 15 minutes

oven temperature: 220°C, 425°F, Gas Mark 7

makes about 30

750 g/1½ lb wholemeal flour

½ teaspoon salt

25 g/1 oz fresh yeast, crumbled

1 teaspoon soft dark brown sugar

25 g/1 oz soya flour

300 ml/½ pint tepid water

150 ml/½ pint homemade yogurt (page 139)

1 tablespoon olive oil

50 g/2 oz wheat sprouts

beaten egg

cracked wheat

1 Put the flour and salt into a warm bowl.
2 Mix the yeast, sugar and soya flour with a little of the tepid water until smooth; beat to dissolve the yeast. Stand in a warm place until the yeast mixture is frothy.
3 Pour the yeast mixture into the flour, adding the remaining tepid water, the yogurt and olive oil; work together to a smooth dough.
4 Knead the dough on a lightly floured surface until smooth and elastic.
5 Put the dough into a lightly floured bowl; cover with a clean cloth and leave in a warm place for 1 hour. Work the wheat sprouts into the dough.
6 Turn the dough onto a lightly floured surface once again; knead briefly for 1–2 minutes. Divide the dough into about thirty even-sized pieces; roll each one into a long thin sausage.
7 Place the strips of dough on greased baking sheets, allowing room for spreading. Leave in a warm place for 10 minutes to rise.
8 Glaze with beaten egg and sprinkle with cracked wheat.
9 Bake in the preheated oven for about 15 minutes until the bread sticks are crisp and golden.
10 Serve warm straight from the oven, or warmed through if made in advance.

Cook's Tip Unlike many bread recipes, this one calls for the dough to be shaped into quite narrow strips. This is easier to do if you roll the dough strips into sausage shapes on a lightly floured work surface.
Variation Sprinkle the bread sticks with sesame seeds instead of cracked wheat.

FLOWER POT SESAME LOAF

preparation: 30 minutes, plus proving

cooking: about 40 minutes

oven temperature: 220°C, 450°F, Gas Mark 8

makes 2 loaves

wholemeal bread dough

(using 750 g/1½ lb flour, page 124)

3 tablespoons sesame seeds

beaten egg

1 Lightly grease two clean clay flower pots, about 15 cm/6 inch across the top in diameter.
2 Make up the wholemeal bread dough as in the recipe for Wholemeal Bread Sticks to stage 5; work in 2 tablespoons of the sesame seeds with the wheat sprouts.
3 Knead the risen dough lightly on a floured work surface and divide into two equal portions; shape into two smooth balls and drop one into each greased flower pot.
4 Cover and leave in a warm place to rise for about 35−40 minutes.
5 Glaze with beaten egg and sprinkle with the remaining sesame seeds.
6 Bake in the preheated oven for about 40 minutes. To test whether the loaves are cooked, turn one out of its flower pot and tap it on the bottom; if it sounds hollow, it is cooked.
7 Cool on a wire rack.

Cook's Tip If you do not have suitable flower pots, 15 cm/6 inch diameter deep cake tins can be used instead.
Variation To make a savoury flower pot loaf, add 2 tablespoons of grated Parmesan cheese to the basic mixture and sprinkle a further tablespoon of cheese over the tops of the shaped loaves before baking.

CHEESE AND POPPY SEED WAFERS

preparation: 20 minutes

cooking: 20 minutes

oven temperature: 200°C, 400°F, Gas Mark 6

makes about 20

100 g/4 oz wholemeal flour

100 g/4 oz plain flour, sifted

1½ teaspoons baking powder

¼ teaspoon celery salt

generous pinch of freshly ground black pepper

50 g/2 oz medium-fat cream cheese

1 tablespoon poppy seeds

3 tablespoons grated Parmesan cheese

about 5 tablespoons skimmed milk

to garnish:

paprika

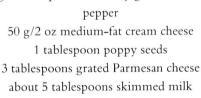

1 Put the wholemeal flour into a bowl; add the plain flour, baking powder, celery salt and pepper. Rub in the cream cheese.
2 Add the poppy seeds and Parmesan cheese and mix to a soft dough with the skimmed milk.
3 Roll out the dough on a lightly floured surface, to about 5 mm/¼ inch thick. Using a fluted square biscuit cutter, cut the dough into about twenty small shapes. Place on lightly greased baking sheets.
4 Bake in the preheated oven for 15−20 minutes, until a rich golden colour and crisp.
5 Remove to a wire rack to cool and dust lightly with paprika.

Cook's Tip The basic dough for the wafers is much easier to roll out and shape if it is made up in advance and chilled for 8 hours.
Variation Use caraway seeds in place of poppy seeds.

LIGHT-AS-AIR LEMON CAKE

preparation: 30 minutes, plus standing

cooking: 12−15 minutes

oven temperature: 180°C, 350°F, Gas Mark 4

serves 6

•

5 eggs, separated

75 g/3 oz golden granulated sugar

75 g/3 oz ground, unblanched almonds

finely grated rind of 2 lemons

filling:

lemon filling (page 128)

2 tablespoons homemade yogurt

(page 139)

to decorate:

icing sugar

thin strips of lemon peel

1 Grease a Swiss roll tin (about 30 × 20 cm/12 × 8 inch) and line it with non-stick silicone or greased greaseproof paper.
2 Put the egg yolks and sugar into a bowl and whisk until the mixture is thick, light and creamy.
3 Whisk the egg whites until stiff but not dry.
4 Whisk the lemon rind into the egg and sugar mixture, and then fold in the egg whites and the ground almonds, lightly but thoroughly.
5 Spread the sponge mixture evenly into the tin. Bake in the preheated oven for 12−15 minutes, until firm but spongy to the touch.
6 Remove the cooked sponge from the oven and immediately cover it with a layer of greaseproof paper and a damp tea towel. Leave in a cool place for 4−6 hours.
7 Dust a piece of greaseproof paper lightly with icing sugar; turn out the sponge cake, peeling off its lining paper. Spread with the lemon filling, and then with the yogurt, and roll up as for a Swiss roll. Do not worry if it cracks slightly.
8 Place on a serving platter; dust with a little extra icing sugar and sprinkle with the strips of lemon peel.

Cook's Tip Press the lining paper well into the edges and corners of the Swiss roll tin so that the baked sponge has a really good shape.
Variation Add some ground ginger to the whisked sponge mixture, omitting the grated lemon rind; add a little chopped stem ginger to the lemon filling.

SHARP LEMON TART

preparation: 20 minutes

cooking: 35 minutes

oven temperature: 190°C, 375°F, Gas Mark 5

serves 6

•

175 g/6 oz Lean Pastry (page 140)

filling:

finely grated rind of 2 lemons

juice of 1 lemon

25 g/1 oz butter

generous pinch of ground nutmeg

25 g/1 oz soft brown sugar

3 eggs

150 ml/¼ pint homemade yogurt (page 139)

1 Roll out the pastry quite thinly and use to line a loose-bottomed fluted flan tin, about 23 cm/9 inch in diameter. Press up the edges well.
2 Make the filling: put the lemon rind and juice, butter, nutmeg and sugar into a pan; stir over a gentle heat until the butter has melted and the sugar has dissolved.
3 Remove from the heat and beat in the eggs and the yogurt; pour into the pastry case.
4 Bake in the preheated oven for about 30 minutes until the filling has just set.
5 Serve warm.

Cook's Tip When lining the tin with the pastry, it is very important to push the edges up well above the rim of the tin; otherwise the lemon filling can seep over the rim during baking.
Variation Limes make an equally tangy filling.

Light-as-Air Lemon Cake: *Not quite a Swiss roll, this lemon sponge cake has a feather-like texture.* **Baked Citrus Cheesecake:** *A sure winner with its refreshing tang of orange.*

BAKED CITRUS CHEESECAKE

preparation: 20 minutes

cooking: about 40 minutes

oven temperature: 180°C, 350°F, Gas Mark 4

serves 6

450 g/1 lb curd cheese

finely grated rind of 1 orange

50 g/2 oz soft brown sugar

3 eggs, beaten

4 tablespoons homemade yogurt

(page 139) or quark

2 tablespoons plain flour

to decorate:

3 tablespoons homemade yogurt

(page 139) or quark

grated orange rind

1 Grease and line a 20 cm/8 inch loose-bottomed cake tin with non-stick silicone or greased greaseproof paper.

2 Beat the curd cheese with the orange rind, sugar, eggs, yogurt or quark and plain flour; spread the mixture evenly in the prepared tin.

3 Bake in the preheated oven for 40 minutes, until just firm and set to the touch.

4 Allow the cheesecake to cool in its tin.

5 Turn the cooled cheesecake onto a flat serving plate. Spread the yogurt or quark evenly over the top and sprinkle with orange rind.

Cook's Tip Baked cheesecakes require a very even oven temperature; it is worth checking your oven with an oven thermometer to see that the thermostat is accurate.

Variation Use other citrus fruits in place of oranges; try lemons, limes or grapefruit.

SPICED PUMPKIN PIE

preparation: 25 minutes

cooking: 45−50 minutes

oven temperature: 180°C, 350°F, Gas Mark 4

serves 6−8

225 g/8 oz Lean Pastry (page 140)

275 g/10 oz cooked and puréed pumpkin

½ teaspoon ground cinnamon

¼ teaspoon ground ginger

75 g/3 oz soft dark brown sugar

3 eggs

2 tablespoons brandy

200 ml/⅓ pint homemade yogurt (page 139)

3 tablespoons chopped pecans or walnuts

1 Roll out the pastry and use to line a fluted, loose-bottomed, round flan tin, 23 cm/9 inch in diameter; press up the edges well.

2 Beat the pumpkin purée with the spices and sugar until smooth; beat in the eggs, brandy, yogurt and half the nuts. Pour the mixture into the pastry case, and sprinkle with the remaining nuts.

3 Bake in the preheated oven for 45−50 minutes until the filling is set and the pastry is pale golden.

4 Serve warm.

Cook's Tip When it is impossible to buy fresh pumpkin, use the canned variety which can be bought without added sugar. For a professional edge to the pastry, brush lightly with beaten egg before pouring in the pumpkin filling.

Variation Raisins or sultanas give a pleasant, natural sweetness to the filling; use 2 tablespoons either instead of or in addition to the nuts.

ALMOND CHEESE SLICES

preparation: 30 minutes

cooking: 35–40 minutes

oven temperature: 190°C, 375°F, Gas Mark 5

makes 8–10

225 g/8 oz Lean Pastry (page 140)

100 g/4 oz dried apricots

3 tablespoons orange juice

175 g/6 oz curd cheese

50 g/2 oz soft dark brown sugar

finely grated rind of ½ orange

few drops of almond essence

3 eggs, separated

3 tablespoons golden granulated sugar

3 tablespoons ground almonds

1 Roll out the pastry quite thinly and use to line a rectangular, fluted, loose-bottomed flan tin, about 10 × 35 cm/4 × 14 inch; press up the edges well.
2 Put the apricots and orange juice into a liquidizer or food processor; blend to a smooth paste. Spread over the base of the pastry case.
3 Beat the curd cheese with the brown sugar, orange rind, almond essence and egg yolks; spread evenly over the apricot mixture.
4 Whisk the egg whites until stiff but not dry, and whisk in the golden granulated sugar; fold in the almonds. Spread the meringue mixture evenly into the pastry case, forking it up decoratively.
5 Bake in the preheated oven for 35–40 minutes. Allow to cool slightly.
6 Serve warm or cold, cut into slices.

Cook's Tip If you do not have a tin of the specified size, roll the pastry out and cut a rectangle to the measurements given. Place on a lightly greased baking sheet, pinch the edges of the pastry to make a rim all the way round and proceed as above.
Variation Substitute a different dried fruit for the apricots, but make sure that it is soft enough to purée.

SWEDISH-STYLE APPLE CAKE

preparation: 15 minutes

cooking: about 45 minutes

oven temperature: 200°C, 400°F, Gas Mark 6

serves 6

100 g/4 oz wholemeal flour

25 g/1 oz soft dark brown sugar

1 egg, beaten

¼ teaspoon mixed spice

150 ml/¼ pint skimmed milk

150 ml/¼ pint homemade yogurt (page 139)

finely grated rind of ½ lemon

450 g/1 lb cooking apples, peeled, cored and sliced

2 tablespoons flaked almonds

1 Grease a shallow ovenproof dish, about 1 litre/1¾ pints in capacity.
2 Put the flour, sugar, egg, spice and milk into a bowl and beat until very smooth; beat in the yogurt and lemon rind.
3 Spread the batter evenly in the greased dish and arrange the sliced apples on the top; sprinkle with the flaked almonds.
4 Bake in the preheated oven for about 45 minutes, until well risen and golden.
5 Serve immediately.
6 Serve with extra homemade yogurt, if liked.

Cook's Tip If you make the batter up about 1 hour in advance and leave it to stand, covered, in the kitchen, it tends to rise better.
Variation Try other seasonal fruits instead of apples, for example, stoned and quartered plums, sliced fresh peaches with their skins or stoned and quartered apricots.

FRESH PINEAPPLE CAKE

preparation: 20 minutes

cooking: 35−40 minutes

oven temperature: 180°C, 350°F, Gas Mark 4

serves 6

3 slices fresh pineapple, chopped

finely grated rind of 1 lemon

3 eggs, separated

75 g/3 oz soft dark brown sugar

75 g/3 oz self-raising wholemeal flour, sifted

pinch of ground ginger

sauce:

150 ml/¼ pint homemade yogurt (page 139)

2 egg yolks

2 tablespoons Marsala

to decorate:

1 tablespoon toasted flaked almonds

1 Grease and line a loose-bottomed cake tin, about 23 cm/9 inch in diameter, with non-stick silicone or greased greaseproof paper.
2 Mix two-thirds of the pineapple with the lemon rind and scatter over the base of the tin.
3 Whisk the egg yolks with the sugar until thick, light and creamy.
4 Whisk the egg whites until stiff but not dry.
5 Fold the flour into the whisked egg and sugar mixture, together with the whisked egg whites and the remaining pineapple.
6 Spread the mixture evenly into the prepared tin. Bake in the preheated oven for 35−40 minutes until firm but spongy to the touch.
7 Meanwhile make the sauce. Put the yogurt, egg yolks and Marsala into a bowl over a pan of hot water; whisk until slightly frothy.
8 Unmould the pineapple cake carefully onto a serving dish; sprinkle with the almonds and serve hot with the whisked sauce.

Cook's Tip If you wish to make the cake in advance, cool it and then wrap in foil. The cake can then be warmed through in a moderate oven, in its foil wrapping.
Variation Well-drained pineapple canned in natural juice can be used in place of fresh pineapple; alternatively, make a peach cake, either using sliced skinned fresh peaches, or well-drained ones canned in natural juice.

DATE AND BRAN BISCUITS

preparation: 10 minutes

cooking: about 20 minutes

oven temperature: 190°C, 375°F, Gas Mark 5

makes about 12

225 g/8 oz rolled oats

4 tablespoons bran flakes

2 tablespoons sesame seeds

2 tablespoons sunflower seeds

175 g/6 oz stoned dates, finely chopped

50 g/2 oz dried figs, finely chopped

4 tablespoons honey

finely grated rind of ½ orange

50 g/2 oz butter

1 egg, beaten

1 Grease and line a Swiss roll tin (about 30 × 20 cm/12 × 8 inch) with non-stick silicone or greased greasproof paper.
2 Mix the rolled oats, bran flakes, sesame seeds, sunflower seeds, dates and figs together in a bowl.
3 Put the honey, orange rind and butter into a pan; stir over a gentle heat until the butter has melted.
4 Stir the melted mixture into the dry ingredients, together with the beaten egg.
5 Spread the mixture evenly in the prepared tin. Bake in the preheated oven for 20 minutes. Mark into twelve squares or rectangles with a sharp knife and leave to cool.
6 Separate the biscuits and store in an airtight tin.

Cook's Tip This mixture needs to be spread into the tin immediately; once it starts to cool, it loses its pliability.
Variation Other dried fruits such as Muscatel raisins or dried apricots can be used.

Fresh Pineapple Cake: *A warm wedge of crumbly pineapple and almond cake is irrestible especially when topped with a cloud of whisked yogurt and Marsala sauce.*

COFFEE PEANUT COOKIES

preparation: 20 minutes

cooking: 20 minutes

oven temperature: 180°C, 350°F, Gas Mark 4

makes about 20

75 g/3 oz butter

100 g/4 oz muscovado sugar

1 egg, beaten

3 tablespoons homemade yogurt (page 139)

250 g/9 oz wholemeal flour, sifted

1 tablespoon instant coffee powder

1 teaspoon baking powder

pinch of salt

50 g/2 oz fresh shelled peanuts, roughly chopped

1 Cream the butter and sugar together until thoroughly mixed.
2 Mix in the beaten egg, yogurt, flour, coffee powder, baking powder and salt. Mix in the peanuts.
3 Put generously rounded teaspoons of the mixture onto greased baking sheets, allowing room for spreading.
4 Bake in the preheated oven for about 20 minutes until golden.
5 Remove to a wire rack to cool.

Cook's Tip If fresh peanuts are difficult to obtain, the dry-roasted variety (although pre-salted) can be soaked in a little tepid water for 10 minutes, then drained thoroughly and crisped in a preheated oven, 190°C/375°F/Gas Mark 5, for 5 minutes.
Variation The cookies also have a very good texture and flavour if chopped, shelled Brazil nuts are used instead of peanuts.

FRESH STRAWBERRY SHORTCAKE

preparation: 30 minutes

cooking: 25 minutes

oven temperature: 190°C, 375°F, Gas Mark 5

serves 6–8

225 g/8 oz self-raising wholemeal flour

generous pinch of salt

50 g/2 oz cornflour

1 tablespoon ground almonds

100 g/4 oz soft dark brown sugar

225 g/8 oz quark

1 egg, beaten

2 tablespoons chopped almonds

sauce:

225 g/8 oz strawberries, chopped

1 tablespoon Cointreau

juice of ½ orange

to decorate:

whole strawberries

crème fraîche

1 Put the flour, salt, cornflour, ground almonds, sugar, quark and beaten egg into a bowl; work the ingredients together quickly to a smooth dough.
2 Press the prepared dough into a rectangular, fluted, loose-bottomed flan tin (about 10 × 35 cm/4 × 14 inch); scatter the almonds over the top.
3 Bake the shortcake in the preheated oven for 25 minutes until risen and pale golden.
4 Meanwhile make the sauce: put the strawberries, Cointreau and orange juice into a liquidizer or food processor; blend until smooth.
5 Immediately the shortcake is taken out of the oven, lift it carefully out of its tin and cut into slices.
6 Serve warm, topping each portion with a little fresh strawberry sauce and a spoonful of crème fraîche, and decorate with a whole strawberry.

Cook's Tip These quantities allow for quite generous portions, and, with extra sauce, the shortcake can be sufficient for ten people.
Variation The shortcake mixture can be pressed into individual loose-bottomed moulds, if preferred. Reduce the cooking time by 5–10 minutes.

GINGER OATCAKES

preparation: 15 minutes

cooking: about 15 minutes

oven temperature: 190°C, 375°F, Gas Mark 5

makes about 12

100 g/4 oz fine oatmeal

100 g/4 oz wholemeal flour

½ teaspoon salt

1 teaspoon ground ginger

100 g/4 oz curd cheese

about 3 tablespoons skimmed milk

2 pieces preserved stem ginger, very finely chopped

1 Put the oatmeal and flour into a bowl with the salt and ground ginger.
2 Add the curd cheese in small pieces and rub into the dry ingredients; bind to a coarse dough with the milk, adding the chopped stem ginger.
3 Roll out the dough on a lightly floured surface to just under 1 cm/½ inch thick. Using a 6 cm/2½ inch plain pastry cutter, cut the dough into circles.
4 Place them on a lightly greased baking sheet, leaving space between each one.
5 Bake in the preheated oven for about 15 minutes, until golden and crisp.
6 Cool on a wire rack before storing in an airtight tin.
7 Serve as an accompaniment to low-fat cheeses, or with yogurt as a quick dessert.

Cook's Tip Wholemeal flours and oatmeal vary considerably in texture and coarseness; you may need extra milk to mix to a dough.
Variation Try adding finely chopped nuts in place of the chopped ginger.

SPECIAL GINGERBREAD

preparation: 20 minutes

cooking: about 1 – 1¼ hours

oven temperature: 180°C, 350°F, Gas Mark 4

makes 1 × 20 cm/8 inch cake

175 g/6 oz honey

grated rind and juice of ½ lemon

1 tablespoon ground ginger

200 ml/⅓ pint homemade yogurt (page 139)

2 eggs, beaten

100 g/4 oz wholemeal flour

50 g/2 oz plain flour

50 g/2 oz ground almonds

2 teaspoons bicarbonate of soda

1 teaspoon baking powder

225 g/8 oz carrots, finely grated

75 g/3 oz raisins

75 g/3 oz dried figs, chopped

50 g/2 oz unblanched almonds, chopped

1 Grease and line a 20 cm/8 inch square cake tin with non-stick silicone or greased greaseproof paper.
2 Put the honey, lemon rind and juice, and the ground ginger into a small pan; stir over a gentle heat until the honey has melted.
3 Remove the pan from the heat and beat in the yogurt and eggs.
4 Put the flours, ground almonds and raising agents into a bowl; add the honey and yogurt mixture and beat until smooth.
5 Mix in the carrots, raisins, figs and almonds. Pour into the prepared tin.
6 Bake in the preheated oven for about 1 – 1¼ hours, until cooked through. Test with a fine skewer.
7 Cool in its tin for a few minutes and then turn the special gingerbread onto a wire rack. Serve cut in squares, either while it is still warm or when cold.

Cook's Tip If you like a really strong ginger flavour, increase the amount of ground ginger by half as much again.
Variation To turn this recipe into a pudding, bake the mixture in a well-greased savarin tin (ring-shaped, with a hole in the centre). Serve warm, cut in portions, with homemade yogurt or crème fraîche.

Accompaniments

The trimmings that help to make a meal are almost as important as the actual dishes: croûtons to serve with soups, dressings for salads and accompanying sauces. They all set that special seal on a meal and show that you really care about detail.

There are also the basic techniques, the culinary tactics that make so much difference to the finished dish. For example, I have created Lean Pastry, using low-calorie curd cheese instead of butter or margarine, for making flan cases and small tartlets. It is a little more elastic than standard shortcrust and needs careful handling; roll it thinly and then leave it to relax for about half an hour before cutting out and shaping. Once baked, it is light and biscuity in texture, but not crumbly.

All the recipes in this chapter will help to give your cooking that light, flavourful quality that is the essence of *Lean Cuisine*; and many can be made well in advance to save time on the day you prepare and serve the meal.

VEGETABLE STOCK

preparation: 10 minutes
cooking: 1½ hours
makes about 1 litre/1¾ pints

3 medium potatoes, peeled and chopped
1 medium onion, peeled and thinly sliced
2 leeks, split, cleaned and chopped
2 celery sticks, chopped
2 medium carrots, peeled and chopped
1 small fennel head, thinly sliced
thyme, parsley stalks, and 2 bay leaves
salt and freshly ground black pepper

1 Put all the vegetables into a pan with the herbs and 1.5 litres/2½ pints water; bring to the boil slowly and skim off the surface scum.
2 Add salt and pepper to taste.
3 Simmer for about 1½ hours, covered, skimming the stock three or four times during cooking.
4 Strain the stock through clean muslin or a very fine sieve.
5 Cool quickly and store in the refrigerator until needed.

Cook's Tip The strained vegetables can be puréed and mixed with some of the prepared stock and some skimmed milk to make a delicious soup.
Variation Use other vegetables such as courgettes, button mushrooms, parsnips and asparagus trimmings. It is important to use a fresh sprig of thyme and a good bunch of parsley stalks for maximum flavour.

FISH STOCK

preparation: 15 minutes
cooking: 35 minutes
makes about 900 ml/1½ pints

900 g/2 lb fish trimmings (bones, skin, etc)
1 small onion, peeled and finely chopped
2 leeks, split, cleaned and chopped
1 bay leaf
parsley stalks, sprig of fennel, lemon peel
1.2 litres/2 pints water
200 ml/⅓ pint dry white wine
salt and freshly ground black pepper

1 Wash the fish trimmings and put them into a pan with the onion, leeks, bay leaf, parsley stalks, fennel, lemon peel and water.
2 Bring to the boil slowly and remove any surface scum.
3 Add the white wine, and salt and pepper to taste.
4 Simmer very gently for 30 minutes; skim the stock once or twice during this time.
5 Strain the stock through clean muslin or a very fine sieve.
6 Cool quickly and keep chilled until required.

Cook's Tip If you do not have the time to make your own fish stock, some very good fish stock cubes are available but they will not give a dish quite the same full flavour.
Variation For a shellfish stock, use prawn shells and trimmings as the base flavouring.

CHICKEN STOCK

preparation: 10 minutes
cooking: 1 hour 40 minutes
makes about 1 litre/1¾ pints

1 boiling fowl, cleaned
bouquet garni
1 small onion, peeled and stuck with
3 cloves
salt and freshly ground black pepper
small bunch of tarragon

1 Put the boiling fowl into a pan with 2 litres/3½ pints water; bring to the boil slowly and remove any surface scum.
2 Add the bouquet garni, the onion studded with the cloves, salt and pepper to taste, and the tarragon.
3 Simmer the stock gently for 1½ hours, skimming the stock regularly.
4 Strain the stock through clean muslin or a very fine sieve.
5 Cool quickly and keep chilled until required.

Cook's Tip As homemade chicken stock has such a good flavour, it is worth freezing in small plastic containers or in ice cube trays for future use.
The cooked chicken flesh can be used for a soup or pâté.
Variation When a roast or boiled chicken has been stripped of its meat, the carcass can be used to make this stock.

TOMATO SAUCE

preparation: 10 minutes

cooking: 30 minutes

makes approximately 400 ml/14 fl oz

1 medium onion, peeled and chopped

2 tablespoons olive oil

750 g/1½ lb tomatoes, skinned

1 tablespoon chopped basil

150 ml/¼ pint red wine

½ teaspoon soft dark brown sugar

salt and freshly ground black pepper

1 tablespoon tomato paste

½ teaspoon grated orange rind

1 Fry the onion gently in the oil for 3 minutes; add the seeded and chopped tomatoes and basil and cook together for a further 2 minutes.
2 Add the remaining ingredients and simmer gently for 25 minutes, until the sauce is soft and pulpy.
3 Press the sauce through a sieve.
4 Reheat the sauce if a hot sauce is required; otherwise cover it and store in a refrigerator.

Cook's Tip This sauce is much easier to sieve if it is first blended in a liquidizer or food processor.
Variation A large garlic clove, peeled and crushed, may also be added to the sauce, if wished. Chicken stock (page 137) can be used instead of the red wine. If you add 175 g/6 oz finely chopped cooked chicken or veal to this basic sauce, it makes a very good accompaniment to cooked pasta.

HERB AND LEMON SAUCE

preparation: 10 minutes

makes about 300 ml/½ pint

2 hard-boiled egg yolks

grated rind and juice of 1 lemon

1 teaspoon French mustard

1 teaspoon soft dark brown sugar

4 tablespoons chicken stock (page 137)

2 tablespoons olive oil

4 tablespoons homemade yogurt (page 139)

1 tablespoon each, chopped tarragon, basil and parsley

salt and freshly ground black pepper

1 Mix the egg yolks to a paste with the lemon rind and juice, mustard, and sugar.
2 Gradually beat in the chicken stock, olive oil and yogurt.
3 Add the herbs, and salt and pepper to taste.

Cook's Tip It is essential to chop the herbs very finely so that they give maximum flavour to the sauce.
Variation Fresh herbs must be used for this sauce; if you cannot obtain tarragon and basil, use 3 tablespoons chopped parsley, mixed with some chopped chives if liked. A large garlic clove, peeled and crushed, may also be added to the sauce, if wished.

BASIL AND GARLIC OIL

preparation: 5 minutes

makes 600 ml/1 pint

4 large garlic cloves, peeled

2 tablespoons basil leaves, chopped

1 teaspoon peppercorns

600 ml/1 pint virgin olive oil

1 Bruise the garlic cloves with the back of a wooden spoon.
2 Put the garlic, basil and peppercorns into a clean bottle; top up with the olive oil and secure the bottle with a stopper.
3 Give the bottle a good shake and keep in a cool place for 1 week before using.

Cook's Tip Although a good quality olive oil is specified in this recipe, the added flavouring is a wonderful way of masking a more inferior olive oil. This flavoured oil is very good for tossing cooked pasta in; you only need 2 teaspoons.
Variation Use any herbs that are readily available; in season rosemary, tarragon and thyme are all good choices.

RASPBERRY VINAIGRETTE

preparation: 5 minutes

makes about 150 ml/¼ pint

3 tablespoons fresh raspberry purée, sieved

juice of 1 orange

3 tablespoons olive oil

2 teaspoons Crème de Cassis

salt and freshly ground black pepper

1 Mix all the ingredients together until thoroughly blended. One of the easiest ways of doing this is to shake all the ingredients in a screw-topped jar.

2 Serve over fruit-based salads, or as a dressing for composite salads such as those containing game or poultry.

Cook's Tip Try serving this fruity dressing over ripe, peeled, halved and cored pears, as a simple starter; the cavities can first be filled with curd cheese and chopped herbs.

Variation Frozen raspberries can be used when the fresh variety is unavailable. A little blackcurrant cordial can be substituted for Crème de Cassis.

YOGURT MAYONNAISE

preparation: 5 minutes

makes about 150 ml/¼ pint

2 egg yolks

150 ml/¼ pint thick homemade yogurt (page 139)

1 teaspoon Dijon mustard

2 teaspoons white wine vinegar

salt and freshly ground black pepper

1 garlic clove, peeled and crushed

1 Beat all the ingredients together until thoroughly mixed; for a very smooth texture do this in a liquidizer or food processor.

Cook's Tip If you wish to keep the mayonnaise in the refrigerator for a day or two, lay a piece of cling film over the surface to prevent a skin from forming.

Variation Chopped herbs can be added to give the mayonnaise a quite different flavour. Add a little curry powder if you are serving it with cold cooked poultry or cold white fish.

HOMEMADE YOGURT

preparation: 10 minutes, plus fermenting

cooking: 1 minute

makes about 600 ml/1 pint

600 ml/1 pint semi-skimmed milk

1½ tablespoons natural low-fat yogurt or homemade yogurt (see Cook's Tip)

1 Put the milk into a pan and bring just to the boil; allow to cool to blood heat.

2 Lightly whisk in the live yogurt until thoroughly mixed.

3 Pour into a wide-necked vacuum flask, and stopper securely.

4 Leave to stand undisturbed for about 10 hours or overnight.

5 The yogurt can then be kept in the refrigerator for up to 4 days.

Cook's Tip It is essential that all the utensils are spotlessly clean. Instead of using a vacuum flask, the yogurt can be made in a covered bowl: pour the milk and yogurt mixture into a bowl; cover with cling film and wrap in a towel or thick cloth; stand in a warm place to ferment, as above.

Use 1½ tablespoons of this yogurt as a starter for your next batch.

Variation To make a thicker-textured yogurt, add 1 tablespoon powdered skimmed milk when you add the live yogurt to the tepid milk.

Add a little fruit purée, some chopped nuts or raisins to a portion of the fermented, homemade yogurt.

FROMAGE BLANC

*preparation: 15 minutes, plus standing and
draining*
cooking: 1 minute
makes about 900 ml/1½ pints

900 ml/1½ pints semi-skimmed milk
2 teaspoons rennet or ¼ of a junket tablet

1 Put the milk into a clean saucepan and heat gently to a temperature at which you can just bear putting your finger into the milk.
2 Remove the pan from the heat, add the rennet or junket tablet and stir until completely blended.
3 Cover and leave to stand at room temperature for 24 hours.
4 Line a colander or large sieve with muslin, and rest over a large bowl, making sure that there is plenty of space between the bottom of the bowl and the base of the colander or sieve.
5 Tip the set junket into the sieve, and leave to drain for about 1 hour, so that the curds separate from the whey.
6 Spoon the set fromage blanc from the sieve into a container. It can be kept, covered, in the refrigerator for up to 4 days.

Cook's Tip If you do not have any muslin, a scalded J-cloth can be used instead.
Variation If full-fat milk is used, it will result in a fromage blanc that is both richer in flavour but higher in calories.

DRY-BAKE HERB CROUTONS

preparation: 10 minutes
cooking: 10−12 minutes
oven temperature: 190°C, 375°F, Gas Mark 5
makes about 24

4 slices wholemeal bread
about 15g/½ oz softened butter
1 tablespoon chopped parsley
1 tablespoon chopped rosemary
salt and freshly ground black pepper
1 tablespoon sesame seeds

1 Spread each slice of bread very lightly with softened butter.
2 Mix the parsley, rosemary, salt and pepper to taste, and sesame seeds together.
3 Sprinkle the mixture evenly over each slice of bread.
4 Cut the crusts off each slice; cut each slice into six small rectangles, or into fancy shapes with cutters.
5 Place the bread shapes on a baking sheet and bake in the preheated oven for 10−12 minutes until crisp and golden.
6 Serve piping hot with soups, as a garnish for fish dishes, or as an accompanying dunk to dishes such as hummus (page 25).

Cook's Tip If you use day-old bread, you will find it easier to cut and shape, whereas very fresh bread tends to tear.
Variation Instead of using the herb topping, sprinkle with garlic granules and paprika.

LEAN PASTRY

preparation: 5 minutes, plus chilling
makes about 350 g/12 oz

100 g/4 oz wholemeal flour
100 g/4 oz plain flour
100 g/4 oz curd cheese
generous pinch of salt
3 tablespoons homemade yogurt (page 139)
2 egg yolks

1 Put the wholemeal flour and plain flour into a liquidizer or food processor with the curd cheese; blend to a fine crumb texture.
2 Beat the salt, yogurt and egg yolks together. Add to the dry ingredients and process until the mixture forms a ball of dough, being careful not to overmix.
3 Wrap in cling film and chill for 1 hour before using.

Cook's Tip Lean Pastry is more elastic than standard shortcrust pastry, and is more prone to losing its shape. Roll out the pastry to the desired size and then leave it to relax for 10 minutes before cutting into the required shape for lining tins.
Variation Although this pastry contains curd cheese, it does not have a savoury cheese flavour. For a really cheesy pastry, add 2 rounded tablespoons grated Parmesan cheese and an extra ½ tablespoon or so of yogurt for mixing.

CURRY POWDER

preparation: 10 minutes
makes about 225 g/8 oz

1 whole cinnamon stick, about
15 cm/6 inch long, broken into pieces
3 tablespoons whole green cardamoms
2 tablespoons cloves
1½ tablespoons cumin seeds
1 tablespoon coriander seeds
2 tablespoons black peppercorns
½ tablespoon ground nutmeg
½ tablespoon cayenne pepper
1½ tablespoons ground turmeric

1 Put all the spices into a mortar and grind with a pestle until quite fine and well balanced. To save time you can do this in a liquidizer or food processor.
2 Store in an airtight jar, away from direct light.
3 The curry powder retains its flavour for up to 4 months.

Cook's Tip Curries should always be tasted from time to time during cooking, to check that the strength is absolutely right; this is particularly important when using a homemade curry powder.
Variation You can mix ready-ground spices together to make the curry powder, but it will not have quite the same pungency of flavour.

MUSTARD FRUIT PICKLE

preparation: 10 minutes
cooking: 5 minutes
makes about 450 g/1 lb

grated rind and juice of 1 lemon
grated rind of 1 orange
2 tablespoons mustard seeds
2.5 cm/1 inch piece of fresh root ginger,
bruised
1 garlic clove, peeled and bruised
6 tablespoons clear honey
175 g/6 oz firm greengages, halved and
stoned
100 g/4 oz fresh apricots, halved and
stoned
100 g/4 oz fresh red or black cherries
1 firm pear, peeled, halved, cored and cut
into wedges
3 fresh figs, quartered

1 Put the lemon rind and juice, orange rind, mustard seeds, ginger, garlic and honey into a pan; stir until well mixed.
2 Stir over a gentle heat until the honey has dissolved; add the prepared fruits, cover and simmer for 5 minutes.
3 Remove from the heat and leave the fruits to cool in the mustard-flavoured syrup.
4 Spoon into a glass container with a lid and store in the refrigerator for up to 4 days.
5 Eat as a preserve with lean cold meats; it is delicious with smoked and cured lean hams.

Cook's Tip It is important that the fruits are ripe yet still firm, as they need to retain their shape and texture. Chill the pickle for at least 8 hours before eating.
Variation For a very tangy pickle, add thin wedges of lime.

INDEX